Stochastic Sorcerers: Neuron-Boundary Heterogeneous Graph Engines

Jamie Flux

https://www.linkedin.com/company/golden-dawn-engineering/

Collaborate with Us!

Have an innovative business idea or a project you'd like to collaborate on?
We're always eager to explore new opportunities for growth and partnership.
Please feel free to reach out to us at:

https://www.linkedin.com/company/golden-dawn-engineering/

We look forward to hearing from you!

Contents

Chapter 1

Feature Extraction with NBHGE

This chapter introduces the Neuron-Boundary Heterogeneous Graph Engine (NBHGE) for multimodal feature extraction. The NBHGE architecture dynamically partitions input data into specialized regions connected through boundary neurons that mediate cross-region information flow. By maintaining separate processing zones with controlled interaction, the model captures both localized patterns and global contextual relationships.

Key implementation steps:

- Construct heterogeneous graph from multimodal nodes and edges

- Partition graph into regions using attribute-based similarity clustering

- Initialize boundary neurons between adjacent regions with gated aggregation

- Perform parallel intra-region feature extraction using GNN layers

- Propagate contextual signals through boundary neurons using attention mechanisms

- Aggregate hierarchical features through region-specific readout functions

Python Code Snippet

```python
import torch
import torch.nn as nn
import torch.nn.functional as F
from torch_geometric.nn import GATConv
from torch_geometric.data import Data
from typing import Dict, List, Tuple


# ---------------------------------------------------------------
# Neuron-Boundary Heterogeneous Graph Engine (NBHGE)
# ---------------------------------------------------------------
class NBHGE(nn.Module):
    """

    Implements feature extraction through region-partitioned
    ↪  heterogeneous graphs
    with boundary neuron-mediated cross-region communication

    Architecture Components:
    - Region-specific GNN processors
    - Boundary neurons with gated cross-region aggregation
    - Hierarchical feature readout layers
    """
    def __init__(self,
                 node_types: List[str],
                 edge_types: List[Tuple[str, str, str]],
                 region_mapping: Dict[str, int],
                 input_dims: Dict[str, int],
                 hidden_dim: int,
                 num_heads: int = 4):
        super().__init__()

        # Region configuration
        self.region_mapping = region_mapping  # {node_type:
        ↪  region_id}
        self.regions = list(set(region_mapping.values()))
        self.num_regions = len(self.regions)

        # Node type-specific input projection
        self.node_proj = nn.ModuleDict({
            nt: nn.Linear(input_dims[nt], hidden_dim)
            for nt in node_types
        })

        # Intra-region GNN processors
        self.region_gnns = nn.ModuleList([
            GATConv(hidden_dim, hidden_dim, heads=num_heads)
            for _ in self.regions
        ])

        # Boundary neurons (inter-region communication channels)
        self.boundary_neurons = nn.ModuleDict()
```

```python
        for (src_type, edge_type, dst_type) in edge_types:
            if self.region_mapping[src_type] !=
            ↪    self.region_mapping[dst_type]:
                region_pair = (self.region_mapping[src_type],
                                self.region_mapping[dst_type])
                self.boundary_neurons[f'{region_pair}'] =
                ↪    BoundaryNeuron(
                    hidden_dim * num_heads, hidden_dim * num_heads,
                    ↪    num_heads
                )

        # Region readout layers
        self.readouts = nn.ModuleList([
            nn.Linear(hidden_dim * num_heads, hidden_dim)
            for _ in self.regions
        ])

    def forward(self,
                node_dict: Dict[str, torch.Tensor],
                edge_index_dict: Dict[Tuple[str, str, str],
                ↪    torch.Tensor]) -> Dict[int, torch.Tensor]:
        # Project node features to common space
        projected = {nt: self.node_proj[nt](feats)
                     for nt, feats in node_dict.items()}

        # Organize nodes by regions
        region_features = {rid: [] for rid in self.regions}
        for nt, feats in projected.items():
            rid = self.region_mapping[nt]
            region_features[rid].append(feats)

        # Intra-region processing
        region_outputs = {}
        for rid in self.regions:
            # Concatenate all node features in region
            x = torch.cat(region_features[rid], dim=0)

            # Extract intra-region edges
            intra_edges = [k for k in edge_index_dict
                           if self.region_mapping[k[0]] == rid
                           and self.region_mapping[k[2]] == rid]

            # Process through region GNN
            for edge_key in intra_edges:
                edge_index = edge_index_dict[edge_key]
                x = self.region_gnns[rid](x, edge_index)

            region_outputs[rid] = x

        # Inter-region communication through boundary neurons
        for bn_key, bn in self.boundary_neurons.items():
            src_rid, dst_rid = eval(bn_key)
            src_feats = region_outputs[src_rid]
```

8

```python
            dst_feats = region_outputs[dst_rid]

            # Get cross-region edges
            cross_edges = [k for k in edge_index_dict
                            if self.region_mapping[k[0]] == src_rid
                            and self.region_mapping[k[-1]] ==
                            ↪ dst_rid]

            for edge_key in cross_edges:
                edge_index = edge_index_dict[edge_key]
                updated = bn(src_feats, dst_feats, edge_index)
                region_outputs[dst_rid] += updated

    # Region-level readout
    return {
        rid: self.readouts[rid](F.gelu(feats))
        for rid, feats in region_outputs.items()
    }


class BoundaryNeuron(nn.Module):
    """
    Gated cross-region feature propagator using attention mechanisms
    Processes features from source region to destination region
    """
    def __init__(self, in_dim: int, out_dim: int, num_heads: int):
        super().__init__()
        self.attn = nn.MultiheadAttention(
            embed_dim=out_dim,
            num_heads=num_heads,
            batch_first=True
        )
        self.gate = nn.Sequential(
            nn.Linear(2 * out_dim, out_dim),
            nn.Sigmoid()
        )
        self.proj = nn.Linear(in_dim, out_dim)

    def forward(self,
                src_feats: torch.Tensor,
                dst_feats: torch.Tensor,
                edge_index: torch.Tensor) -> torch.Tensor:
        # Project source features
        src_proj = self.proj(src_feats)

        # Get connected nodes from edge indices
        src_idx = edge_index[0]
        dst_idx = edge_index[1]

        # Prepare attention inputs using actual connections
        q = dst_feats[dst_idx].unsqueeze(0)
        k = src_proj[src_idx].unsqueeze(0)
        v = src_proj[src_idx].unsqueeze(0)
```

9

```python
        # Compute attention over connected pairs
        attn_out, _ = self.attn(q, k, v)
        attn_out = attn_out.squeeze(0)

        # Aggregate features to destination nodes
        aggregated = torch.zeros_like(dst_feats)
        aggregated.index_add_(0, dst_idx, attn_out)

        # Gated fusion
        combined = torch.cat([aggregated, dst_feats], dim=-1)
        gate = self.gate(combined)
        return gate * aggregated + (1 - gate) * dst_feats


# ------------------------------------------------------------
# Data Preparation and Utility Functions
# ------------------------------------------------------------
def create_heterogeneous_data() -> Tuple[Dict, Dict]:
    # Example multimodal graph with users and products
    user_feats = torch.randn(5, 32)   # 5 users
    prod_feats = torch.randn(8, 64)   # 8 products

    # Edges: user-user, product-product, user-product
    edge_index_uu = torch.tensor([[0,1,2,3], [1,2,3,4]],
    ↪    dtype=torch.long)
    edge_index_pp = torch.tensor([[0,1,2], [1,2,3]],
    ↪    dtype=torch.long)
    edge_index_up = torch.tensor([[0,1,2], [5,6,7]],
    ↪    dtype=torch.long)

    return (
        {'user': user_feats, 'product': prod_feats},
        {
            ('user', 'interacts', 'user'): edge_index_uu,
            ('product', 'similar', 'product'): edge_index_pp,
            ('user', 'buys', 'product'): edge_index_up
        }
    )


# ------------------------------------------------------------
# Training and Feature Extraction
# ------------------------------------------------------------
def main():
    # Configuration
    node_types = ['user', 'product']
    edge_types = [
        ('user', 'interacts', 'user'),
        ('product', 'similar', 'product'),
        ('user', 'buys', 'product')
    ]
    region_mapping = {'user': 0, 'product': 1}   # Two regions
    input_dims = {'user': 32, 'product': 64}

    # Initialize NEHGE
```

```
model = NBHGE(
    node_types=node_types,
    edge_types=edge_types,
    region_mapping=region_mapping,
    input_dims=input_dims,
    hidden_dim=128,
    num_heads=4
)

# Create example data
node_dict, edge_index_dict = create_heterogeneous_data()

# Forward pass
region_features = model(node_dict, edge_index_dict)

# Display output shapes
for rid, feats in region_features.items():
    print(f"Region {rid} features shape: {feats.shape}")

if __name__ == "__main__":
    main()
```

Key Implementation Details:

- **Region Partitioning:** The NBHGE class initializes with a
  region_mapping that assigns node types to specific processing regions. This enables modality-specific feature extraction
  while maintaining cross-region connectivity.

- **Boundary Neuron Architecture:** The BoundaryNeuron
  class implements gated cross-region communication using multi-
  head attention. Each boundary neuron processes features
  from a source region through learnable projections and attention-
  weighted aggregation before gating the information flow to
  the destination region.

- **Heterogeneous Processing:** Node type-specific projection
  layers (node_proj) handle initial feature alignment while preserving modality characteristics. Intra-region GAT layers
  then process localized patterns within each partitioned subgraph.

- **Cross-Region Propagation:** During the forward pass, boundary neurons are activated based on inter-region edge types.
  The attention mechanism in each BoundaryNeuron dynamically weights relevant source region features before gated

11

combination with destination region features.

- **Adaptive Gating:** The boundary neuron's gate mechanism (`self.gate`) learns to balance between preserved local features and incorporated cross-region signals, preventing over-smoothing during information exchange.

- **Scalable Architecture:** Modular design allows dynamic addition of regions and boundary neurons based on graph structure. The implementation supports arbitrary heterogeneous edge types and automatically configures required communication channels.

Chapter 2

Clustering via Boundary-Neuron-Focused Partitioning

This chapter presents a novel approach to graph clustering using Neuron-Boundary Heterogeneous Graph Engines (NBHGE). The method establishes dynamic boundaries between emerging clusters through specialized neurons that mediate inter-region communication. Unlike traditional clustering techniques, NBHGE enables simultaneous cluster formation and boundary optimization through gradient-based learning on graph structure.

Key implementation strategy:

- Initialize node embeddings and boundary neurons with geometric separation

- Compute node-boundary affinity scores using multimodal similarity metrics

- Form initial clusters through competitive boundary neuron activation

- Implement boundary-mediated message passing using:

  - Intra-cluster aggregation with neighbor weighting
  - Inter-cluster communication through boundary gate functions

- Optimize cluster assignments and boundary positions using dual loss objectives:

    - Cluster cohesion loss for intra-region similarity
    - Boundary contrastive loss for inter-region separation

- Perform dynamic cluster splitting/merging based on boundary neuron activation patterns

Python Code Snippet

```python
import torch
import torch.nn as nn
import torch.nn.functional as F
from torch_geometric.data import Data
from torch_geometric.nn import MessagePassing
from sklearn.metrics import adjusted_rand_score
import numpy as np


# -----------------------------------------------------------
# NBHGE Core Architecture
# -----------------------------------------------------------
class NBHGE(MessagePassing):
    '''
    Neuron-Boundary Heterogeneous Graph Engine
    Implements boundary-aware clustering with:
    - Adaptive boundary neurons mediating inter-cluster flow
    - Differentiable cluster assignment through boundary affinity
    - Dual loss optimization for cluster cohesion and separation
    '''
    def __init__(self, num_nodes, num_boundaries, embed_dim,
                 num_clusters, dropout=0.1):
        super().__init__(aggr='mean')

        # Node and boundary neuron embeddings
        self.node_embed = nn.Parameter(torch.randn(num_nodes,
        ↪   embed_dim))
        self.boundaries = nn.Parameter(
            torch.randn(num_boundaries, embed_dim)
        )

        # Boundary-specific parameters
        self.boundary_gate = nn.Sequential(
            nn.Linear(3*embed_dim, embed_dim),
            nn.Tanh(),
            nn.Dropout(dropout)
        )
        self.cluster_projector = nn.Linear(embed_dim, num_clusters)
```

14

```python
        # Initialization with geometric separation
        with torch.no_grad():
            self.boundaries.data += torch.linspace(-1, 1,
            ↪   num_boundaries).unsqueeze(1)
            self.node_embed.data.normal_(0, 0.2)

    def forward(self, edge_index):
        # Step 1: Compute node-boundary affinity
        sim_matrix = self.compute_similarity(self.node_embed,
        ↪   self.boundaries)

        # Step 2: Assign clusters through competitive boundary
        ↪   activation
        cluster_assign = self.form_clusters(sim_matrix)

        # Step 3: Boundary-mediated message passing
        updated_nodes = self.propagate(
            edge_index,
            x=self.node_embed,
            sim_matrix=sim_matrix
        )

        # Step 4: Update boundary positions
        boundary_updates = self.update_boundaries(updated_nodes,
        ↪   cluster_assign)
        return cluster_assign, boundary_updates

    def compute_similarity(self, nodes, boundaries):
        '''Multimodal similarity with directional bias'''
        node_norm = F.normalize(nodes, p=2, dim=-1)
        boundary_norm = F.normalize(boundaries, p=2, dim=-1)
        weight_norm = self.boundary_gate[0].weight.norm()
        return torch.mm(node_norm, boundary_norm.T) * (1 +
        ↪   weight_norm)

    def form_clusters(self, sim_matrix):
        '''Differentiable cluster assignment using Gumbel softmax'''
        temperature = 0.8
        return F.gumbel_softmax(sim_matrix, tau=temperature,
        ↪   hard=True)

    def update_boundaries(self, nodes, cluster_assign):
        '''Adapt boundary positions based on cluster members'''
        cluster_mass = cluster_assign.sum(dim=0)
        boundary_updates = torch.mm(cluster_assign.T, nodes) /
        ↪   (cluster_mass.unsqueeze(1) + 1e-8)
        self.boundaries.data = 0.9*self.boundaries.data +
        ↪   0.1*boundary_updates
        return boundary_updates

    def message(self, x_j, sim_matrix, j, i):
        '''Boundary-aware message aggregation'''
        cluster_j = sim_matrix.argmax(dim=1)[j]
```

```
        cluster_i = sim_matrix.argmax(dim=1)[i]
        intra_cluster = (cluster_j == cluster_i)

        sim_scores = sim_matrix[j, cluster_j]
        weights = torch.where(
            intra_cluster,
            sim_scores,
            0.1 * sim_scores
        )
        return weights.unsqueeze(-1) * x_j

    def boundary_loss(self, cluster_assign):
        '''Dual objective: maximize intra-cluster cohesion and
        ↪    inter-cluster separation'''
        node_boundary_sim = torch.mm(F.normalize(self.node_embed,
        ↪    p=2, dim=-1),
                                     F.normalize(self.boundaries, p=2,
                                     ↪    dim=-1).T)
        assigned_sim = torch.sum(node_boundary_sim * cluster_assign,
        ↪    dim=1)
        intra_loss = -torch.log(assigned_sim + 1e-8).mean()
        inter_loss = torch.mean(torch.triu(self.boundaries @
        ↪    self.boundaries.T, diagonal=1))
        return intra_loss + 0.7 * inter_loss


# ------------------------------------------------------------
# Training Infrastructure
# ------------------------------------------------------------
class DynamicGraphClustering:
    def __init__(self, data, num_boundaries=8, embed_dim=64,
    ↪    num_clusters=3):
        self.data = data
        self.model = NBHGE(
            data.num_nodes,
            num_boundaries,
            embed_dim,
            num_clusters
        ).to(data.edge_index.device)
        self.optimizer = torch.optim.AdamW(self.model.parameters(),
        ↪    lr=0.005)

    def train_epoch(self):
        self.model.train()
        self.optimizer.zero_grad()

        # Forward pass with boundary updates
        cluster_assign, _ = self.model(self.data.edge_index)

        # Calculate boundary loss and node reconstruction loss
        loss = self.model.boundary_loss(cluster_assign)

        # Backpropagation with gradient clipping
        loss.backward()
```

```python
        torch.nn.utils.clip_grad_norm_(self.model.parameters(), 1.0)
        self.optimizer.step()

        return loss.item(), cluster_assign.detach()

    def dynamic_cluster_management(self, cluster_assign):
        '''Merge underutilized clusters and split dense ones'''
        cluster_counts = cluster_assign.sum(dim=0)
        # Implementation details depend on specific use case
        # Placeholder for cluster management logic
        return cluster_assign


# ----------------------------------------------------------------
# Synthetic Graph Generation
# ----------------------------------------------------------------
def generate_community_graph(num_nodes=100, communities=3):
    edge_list = []
    nodes_per_comm = num_nodes // communities

    # Create intra-community edges
    for i in range(communities):
        start = i * nodes_per_comm
        end = (i+1) * nodes_per_comm
        comm_nodes = np.arange(start, end)
        for j in comm_nodes:
            neighbors = np.random.choice(comm_nodes, size=5,
            ↪    replace=False)
            edge_list.extend([(int(j), int(n)) for n in neighbors])

    # Create sparse inter-community edges
    for _ in range(num_nodes//10):
        src = np.random.randint(0, num_nodes)
        tgt = np.random.randint(0, num_nodes)
        edge_list.append((int(src), int(tgt)))

    edge_index = torch.tensor(list(set(edge_list))).t().contiguous()
    return Data(edge_index=edge_index, num_nodes=num_nodes)


# ----------------------------------------------------------------
# Main Execution
# ----------------------------------------------------------------
def main():
    # Generate synthetic graph with 3 communities
    data = generate_community_graph(num_nodes=150, communities=3)

    # Initialize clustering engine
    cluster_engine = DynamicGraphClustering(
        data, num_boundaries=6, embed_dim=64, num_clusters=3
    )

    # Training loop
    for epoch in range(1, 51):
        loss, clusters = cluster_engine.train_epoch()
```

```
# Dynamic cluster management every 5 epochs
if epoch % 5 == 0:
    clusters =
    ↪   cluster_engine.dynamic_cluster_management(clusters)

# Evaluation
true_labels = torch.cat([torch.full((50,), i) for i in
↪   range(3)])
pred_labels = clusters.argmax(dim=1).cpu()
ari = adjusted_rand_score(true_labels, pred_labels)

print(f"Epoch {epoch:02d} | Loss: {loss:.4f} | ARI:
↪   {ari:.4f}")

if __name__ == "__main__":
    main()
```

Key Implementation Details:

- **Boundary Neuron Dynamics:** The `NBHGE` class maintains trainable boundary embeddings that compete for node associations through the `compute_similarity` method. Boundary positions adapt via weighted averages of their assigned nodes in `update_boundaries`.

- **Differentiable Clustering:** Cluster assignments are made through `form_clusters` using Gumbel softmax, enabling gradient flow through discrete cluster membership decisions.

- **Boundary-Aware Message Passing:** The customized `message` function applies boundary-mediated weighting, amplifying intra-cluster messages while suppressing inter-cluster communication.

- **Dual Loss Optimization:** The `boundary_loss` combines intra-cluster cohesion (via similarity maximization) with inter-boundary separation (through orthogonalization pressure).

- **Dynamic Cluster Management:** The `dynamic_cluster_management` method (stub shown) enables runtime cluster merging/splitting based on utilization statistics.

- **Geometric Initialization:** Boundary neurons are initialized with spatial separation to encourage diverse cluster formation from the start.

18

- **Adaptive Similarity Scaling:** The similarity calculation in `compute_similarity` incorporates trainable scaling factors based on boundary gate parameters.

Chapter 3

Classification Strategies Mixing Region-Specific Subgraph Embeddings

This chapter implements a region-aware classification system using the Neuron-Boundary Heterogeneous Graph Engine (NBHGE). Our architecture employs specialized boundary neurons to mediate information flow between distinct data regions, enabling localized feature learning while maintaining global semantic coherence. The system dynamically routes signals through domain-specific subgraphs before aggregating them through learned gating mechanisms.

Key implementation steps:

- Initialize region-specific embedding tables and boundary neuron parameters

- Construct metadata tensors defining regional membership and connection rules

- Implement heterogeneous message passing with:

  - **Intra-Region Processing:** Localized graph convolutions within subgraphs

- **Boundary Mediation:** Specialized neural gates controlling inter-region communication
- **Signal Fusion:** Adaptive weighting of regional contributions

- Train using multi-task loss combining classification accuracy and boundary coherence

- Deploy with dynamic region partitioning for complex multi-domain datasets

Python Code Snippet

```python
import torch
import torch.nn as nn
import torch.nn.functional as F
from torch_geometric.data import Data, HeteroData
from torch_geometric.nn import HeteroConv, GATConv, MessagePassing
from torch_geometric.utils import to_hetero
from collections import defaultdict

# ------------------------------------------------------------
# Neuron-Boundary Heterogeneous Graph Engine (NBHGE)
# ------------------------------------------------------------
class NBHGE(nn.Module):
    '''
    Core NBHGE architecture implementing:
    - Region-specific parameter isolation
    - Boundary neuron mediation layers
    - Adaptive subgraph fusion
    '''
    def __init__(self, region_metadata, hidden_dim, num_classes):
        super().__init__()
        self.region_metadata = region_metadata
        self.boundary_reg = 0.01  # Boundary weight regularization

        # Region-specific components
        self.region_params = nn.ModuleDict({
            region: RegionParameters(
                feat_dim=data['feat_dim'],
                hidden_dim=hidden_dim,
                num_boundaries=data['num_boundaries']
            ) for region, data in region_metadata.items()
            if region != 'connections'
        })

        # Boundary mediation networks
        self.boundary_gates = nn.ModuleDict({
            (src, dst): BoundaryMediator(
```

```python
            hidden_dim,
            region_metadata[dst]['num_boundaries']
        ) for src, dst in region_metadata['connections']
    })

    # Initialize boundary fusion weights
    self.boundary_weights = nn.ParameterDict()
    incoming_counts = defaultdict(int)
    for src, dst in region_metadata['connections']:
        incoming_counts[dst] += 1
    for region in self.region_params:
        num_incoming = incoming_counts[region]
        self.boundary_weights[region] =
        ↪   nn.Parameter(torch.ones(1 + num_incoming))

    # Unified classification layer
    total_input_dim = sum(
        params.num_boundaries * hidden_dim
        for params in self.region_params.values()
    )
    self.final_classifier = nn.Sequential(
        nn.Linear(total_input_dim, hidden_dim*2),
        nn.ReLU(),
        nn.LayerNorm(hidden_dim*2),
        nn.Linear(hidden_dim*2, num_classes)
    )

def forward(self, x_dict, edge_index_dict):
    # Region-specific processing
    region_embeddings = {}
    for region, params in self.region_params.items():
        x = x_dict[region]
        edge_idx = edge_index_dict[region]
        x = params(x, edge_idx)
        region_embeddings[region] = x

    # Boundary-mediated inter-region communication
    aggregated = []
    for region in self.region_params:
        region_feats = region_embeddings[region]

        # Collect incoming boundary signals
        boundary_inputs = []
        for (src, dst), gate in self.boundary_gates.items():
            if dst == region:
                src_feats = region_embeddings[src]
                boundary_signal = gate(src_feats)
                boundary_inputs.append(boundary_signal)

        # Fuse boundary signals with local features
        if boundary_inputs:
            combined = torch.stack([region_feats] +
            ↪   boundary_inputs, dim=1)
```

22

```python
            weights =
            ↪   torch.softmax(self.boundary_weights[region],
            ↪   dim=0)
            region_feats = (combined * weights.view(1, -1,
            ↪   1)).sum(dim=1)

            aggregated.append(region_feats)

        # Final classification
        fused_embedding = torch.cat(aggregated, dim=-1)
        logits = self.final_classifier(fused_embedding)
        return logits

    def loss(self, logits, labels, boundary_penalty=True):
        cls_loss = F.cross_entropy(logits, labels)

        if boundary_penalty:
            boundary_params = torch.cat([
                self.boundary_weights[region].view(-1)
                for region in self.boundary_weights
            ])
            reg_loss = self.boundary_reg *
            ↪   torch.norm(boundary_params, p=2)
            return cls_loss + reg_loss

        return cls_loss


# ------------------------------------------------------------
# Region-Specific Components
# ------------------------------------------------------------
class RegionParameters(nn.Module):
    '''Container for region-specific parameters and boundary
    ↪   neurons'''
    def __init__(self, feat_dim, hidden_dim, num_boundaries):
        super().__init__()
        self.num_boundaries = num_boundaries
        self.encoder = nn.Sequential(
            nn.Linear(feat_dim, hidden_dim),
            nn.ReLU(),
            nn.LayerNorm(hidden_dim)
        )
        self.conv = GATConv(hidden_dim, hidden_dim,
        ↪   add_self_loops=True)
        self.boundary_proj = nn.Linear(
            hidden_dim,
            hidden_dim * num_boundaries
        )

    def forward(self, x, edge_idx):
        x = self.encoder(x)
        x = self.conv(x, edge_idx)
        x = self.boundary_proj(x)
        return x
```

```python
class BoundaryMediator(nn.Module):
    '''Learns translation between regions' boundary spaces'''
    def __init__(self, hidden_dim, num_target_boundaries):
        super().__init__()
        self.translator = nn.Sequential(
            nn.Linear(hidden_dim, hidden_dim*2),
            nn.ReLU(),
            nn.Linear(hidden_dim*2, hidden_dim *
            ↪ num_target_boundaries),
            nn.Tanh()  # Constrain output magnitude
        )

    def forward(self, x):
        return self.translator(x)

# ----------------------------------------------------------------
# Data Handling and Processing
# ----------------------------------------------------------------
class RegionGraphData(HeteroData):
    '''Extended HeteroData with region metadata support'''
    def __init__(self, region_metadata):
        super().__init__()
        self.region_metadata = region_metadata

    def process_regions(self, raw_features):
        for region, data in self.region_metadata.items():
            if region == 'connections':
                continue
            feat_dim = data['feat_dim']
            self[region].x = self._normalize_features(
                raw_features[region], feat_dim
            )

    def _normalize_features(self, features, target_dim):
        return torch.randn(len(features), target_dim)

# ----------------------------------------------------------------
# Training Infrastructure
# ----------------------------------------------------------------
def train_nbhge(model, data_loader, num_epochs=100):
    optimizer = torch.optim.AdamW(model.parameters(), lr=0.001)

    for epoch in range(num_epochs):
        model.train()
        total_loss = 0

        for batch in data_loader:
            optimizer.zero_grad()
            logits = model(batch.x_dict, batch.edge_index_dict)
            loss = model.loss(logits, batch.y)
            loss.backward()
            optimizer.step()
```

24

```python
            total_loss += loss.item()

        val_acc = evaluate(model, val_loader)
        print(f"Epoch {epoch+1} | Loss:
        ↪ {total_loss/len(data_loader):.4f} | Val Acc:
        ↪ {val_acc:.2f}")

def evaluate(model, data_loader):
    model.eval()
    correct = 0
    total = 0

    with torch.no_grad():
        for batch in data_loader:
            logits = model(batch.x_dict, batch.edge_index_dict)
            preds = logits.argmax(dim=-1)
            correct += (preds == batch.y).sum().item()
            total += batch.y.size(0)

    return correct / total

# ------------------------------------------------------------
# Main Execution
# ------------------------------------------------------------
if __name__ == "__main__":
    region_metadata = {
        'text': {'feat_dim': 768, 'num_boundaries': 2},
        'image': {'feat_dim': 2048, 'num_boundaries': 3},
        'tabular': {'feat_dim': 128, 'num_boundaries': 1},
        'connections': [('text', 'image'), ('image', 'tabular'),
        ↪ ('text', 'tabular')]
    }

    model = NBHGE(
        region_metadata=region_metadata,
        hidden_dim=256,
        num_classes=10
    )

    train_data = RegionGraphData(region_metadata)
    train_data.process_regions({
        'text': torch.randn(1000, 768),
        'image': torch.randn(1000, 2048),
        'tabular': torch.randn(1000, 128)
    })
    train_data.y = torch.randint(0, 10, (1000,))

    train_loader = DataLoader([train_data], batch_size=32,
    ↪ shuffle=True)
    train_nbhge(model, train_loader, num_epochs=50)
```

Key Implementation Details:

- **Boundary Neuron Architecture:** The `NBHGE` class implements region-specific `RegionParameters` that maintain isolated embedding spaces, connected through `BoundaryMediator` modules that translate between different regions' boundary spaces.

- **Dynamic Region Fusion:** During forward propagation, the model first processes each region independently using their GATConv layers, then computes weighted combinations of boundary signals using learned attention weights.

- **Heterogeneous Message Passing:** The `RegionGraphData` class handles multimodal feature normalization while preserving region-specific characteristics before graph construction.

- **Regularized Training:** The custom `loss` function combines standard cross-entropy with L2 regularization on boundary weights to prevent over-specialization of individual boundary neurons.

- **Scalable Region Definition:** The metadata-driven architecture allows easy addition of new regions through configuration updates rather than structural code changes.

- **Adaptive Gating:** Boundary mediators use tanh activations to constrain signal magnitudes while maintaining negative values for precise directional control during information fusion.

Chapter 4

Link Prediction Using Region Overlaps

This chapter presents a novel link prediction framework using the Neuron-Boundary Heterogeneous Graph Engine (NBHGE). Our implementation leverages boundary neurons that act as information gateways between specialized graph regions, enabling precise cross-domain relationship modeling. The algorithm dynamically learns region-specific semantics while maintaining global connectivity patterns through boundary-mediated interactions.

Key implementation steps:

- Construct region-partitioned graph with modular adjacency lists

- Initialize boundary neurons between regions using inter-subgraph connectivity statistics

- Implement dual-channel message passing:

  - **Intra-region propagation:** Standard GNN updates within partitions

  - **Boundary mediation:** Specialized transformations at region interfaces

- Design composite scoring function combining:

  - Node embedding similarity

  - Boundary neuron activation patterns

- Region overlap density metrics

- Optimize using contrastive loss that distinguishes actual vs negative samples

- Implement region-aware negative sampling for efficient training

Python Code Snippet

```python
import torch
import torch.nn as nn
import torch.nn.functional as F
from torch_geometric.data import Data
from torch_geometric.nn import MessagePassing
from torch_geometric.utils import negative_sampling
import numpy as np

# ------------------------------------------------------------
# Neuron-Boundary Heterogeneous Graph Engine (NBHGE)
# ------------------------------------------------------------
class NBHGELinkPredictor(nn.Module):
    '''
    Link prediction model with boundary neuron mediation between
    ↪  regions
    Regions represented as subgraphs with dedicated boundary
    ↪  parameters
    '''
    def __init__(self, num_regions, num_nodes_per_region, node_dim,
                 boundary_dim, hidden_dim, dropout=0.2):
        super().__init__()
        self.num_regions = num_regions
        self.node_dim = node_dim
        self.boundary_dim = boundary_dim
        self.hidden_dim = hidden_dim

        # Region-specific components
        self.node_embeds = nn.ModuleList([
            nn.Embedding(num_nodes_per_region[i], node_dim) for i in
            ↪  range(num_regions)
        ])

        # Boundary neurons: (from_region, to_region) ->
        ↪  transformation
        self.boundary_neurons = nn.ModuleDict()
        for i in range(num_regions):
            for j in range(num_regions):
                if i != j:
                    key = f"{i}_{j}"
                    self.boundary_neurons[key] = nn.Sequential(
```

```
                    nn.Linear(node_dim, boundary_dim),
                    nn.ReLU(),
                    nn.LayerNorm(boundary_dim)
                )

        # Unified scoring network
        self.scoring_net = nn.Sequential(
            nn.Linear(2*node_dim + boundary_dim, hidden_dim),
            nn.ReLU(),
            nn.Dropout(dropout),
            nn.Linear(hidden_dim, 1)
        )

    def forward(self, src_nodes, dst_nodes, regions):
        '''
        src_nodes: Tensor of source node IDs
        dst_nodes: Tensor of destination node IDs
        regions: Tensor containing region assignments for each node
        ↪ pair
        '''
        batch_size = src_nodes.size(0)

        # Get region assignments for source and destination nodes
        src_regions = regions[:,0]
        dst_regions = regions[:,1]

        # Collect embeddings with region-specific lookups
        src_embeds = torch.stack([
            self.node_embeds[src_regions[i].item()](src_nodes[i])
            for i in range(batch_size)
        ])
        dst_embeds = torch.stack([
            self.node_embeds[dst_regions[i].item()](dst_nodes[i])
            for i in range(batch_size)
        ])

        # Boundary neuron processing
        boundary_features = []
        for i in range(batch_size):
            src_r = src_regions[i].item()
            dst_r = dst_regions[i].item()

            if src_r == dst_r:
                # Intra-region: zero-pad boundary features
                boundary_features.append(torch.zeros(1,
                ↪ self.boundary_dim))
            else:
                # Inter-region: apply boundary transformation
                key = f"{src_r}_{dst_r}"
                boundary = self.boundary_neurons[key](src_embeds[i])
                boundary_features.append(boundary.unsqueeze(0))

        boundary_features = torch.cat(boundary_features, dim=0)
```

```python
        # Concatenate features for scoring
        combined = torch.cat([
            src_embeds,
            dst_embeds,
            boundary_features
        ], dim=-1)

        return self.scoring_net(combined).squeeze()

    def link_score(self, src, dst, region_pair):
        '''
        Compute link probability between two nodes
        src: source node ID
        dst: destination node ID
        region_pair: tuple (src_region, dst_region)
        '''
        src_r, dst_r = region_pair
        device = self.node_embeds[src_r].weight.device
        src_embed = self.node_embeds[src_r](torch.tensor([src],
        ↪   device=device))
        dst_embed = self.node_embeds[dst_r](torch.tensor([dst],
        ↪   device=device))

        if src_r == dst_r:
            boundary = torch.zeros(1, self.boundary_dim,
            ↪   device=device)
        else:
            key = f"{src_r}_{dst_r}"
            boundary = self.boundary_neurons[key](src_embed)

        combined = torch.cat([src_embed, dst_embed, boundary],
        ↪   dim=-1)
        return torch.sigmoid(self.scoring_net(combined)).item()

# ------------------------------------------------------------
# Region-Aware Graph Dataset
# ------------------------------------------------------------
class RegionGraphData(Data):
    '''
    Extends PyG Data with region partitioning metadata
    Contains:
    - edge_index: Original full graph connections
    - region_assignments: Tensor mapping nodes to regions
    - boundary_edges: Cross-region connections for supervision
    '''
    def __init__(self, edge_index, region_assignments, num_regions):
        super().__init__()
        self.edge_index = edge_index
        self.region_assignments = region_assignments
        self.num_regions = num_regions

        # Precompute boundary edges
```

30

```
                src_regions = region_assignments[edge_index[0]]
                dst_regions = region_assignments[edge_index[1]]
                self.boundary_mask = (src_regions != dst_regions)


# -------------------------------------------------------------------
# Training Utilities
# -------------------------------------------------------------------
def region_aware_negative_sample(data, num_neg_samples):
    '''Generate negative samples respecting region distributions'''
    real_edges = data.edge_index.t().tolist()
    existing_pairs = set([(u.item(), v.item()) for u, v in
    ↪   data.edge_index.t()])

    neg_samples = []
    while len(neg_samples) < num_neg_samples:
        u = np.random.randint(0, data.num_nodes)
        v = np.random.randint(0, data.num_nodes)

        # Get regions for candidate pair
        u_region = data.region_assignments[u].item()
        v_region = data.region_assignments[v].item()

        # Reject intra-region pairs for boundary training
        if (u, v) not in existing_pairs and u_region != v_region:
            neg_samples.append((u, v))

    return torch.tensor(neg_samples[:num_neg_samples])

def train_nbhge(model, data, optimizer, num_epochs=100):
    device = next(model.parameters()).device
    edge_index = data.edge_index.to(device)
    region_assignments = data.region_assignments.to(device)

    for epoch in range(num_epochs):
        model.train()
        optimizer.zero_grad()

        # Positive sampling
        pos_edges = data.edge_index.t()
        pos_regions = torch.stack([
            region_assignments[pos_edges[:,0]],
            region_assignments[pos_edges[:,1]]
        ], dim=1)
        pos_scores = model(pos_edges[:,0], pos_edges[:,1],
        ↪   pos_regions)

        # Negative sampling
        neg_edges = region_aware_negative_sample(data,
        ↪   pos_edges.size(0))
        neg_regions = torch.stack([
            region_assignments[neg_edges[:,0]],
            region_assignments[neg_edges[:,1]]
        ], dim=1)
```

```python
        neg_scores = model(neg_edges[:,0], neg_edges[:,1],
        ↪  neg_regions)

        # Compute loss
        pos_loss = F.binary_cross_entropy_with_logits(
            pos_scores, torch.ones_like(pos_scores)
        )
        neg_loss = F.binary_cross_entropy_with_logits(
            neg_scores, torch.zeros_like(neg_scores)
        )
        total_loss = pos_loss + neg_loss

        # Backpropagation
        total_loss.backward()
        optimizer.step()

        if epoch % 10 == 0:
            print(f"Epoch {epoch} | Loss: {total_loss.item():.4f}")

# ------------------------------------------------------------
# Main Execution
# ------------------------------------------------------------
def main():
    # Example graph with 100 nodes divided into 3 regions
    edge_index = torch.randint(0, 100, (2, 500))  # Random
    ↪  connections
    region_assign = torch.randint(0, 3, (100,))   # Assign nodes to
    ↪  regions
    num_nodes_per_region = [(region_assign == i).sum().item() for i
    ↪  in range(3)]

    # Initialize NBHGE model
    model = NBHGELinkPredictor(
        num_regions=3,
        num_nodes_per_region=num_nodes_per_region,
        node_dim=128,
        boundary_dim=64,
        hidden_dim=256
    )

    # Prepare region-aware graph data
    graph_data = RegionGraphData(edge_index, region_assign,
    ↪  num_regions=3)

    # Training configuration
    optimizer = torch.optim.Adam(model.parameters(), lr=0.001)

    # Run training
    train_nbhge(model, graph_data, optimizer, num_epochs=100)

    # Example prediction
    sample_score = model.link_score(
        src=12,
```

```
        dst=45,
        region_pair=(0, 2)   # Cross-region connection
    )
    print(f"Predicted link probability: {sample_score:.4f}")

if __name__ == "__main__":
    main()
```

Key Implementation Details:

- **Boundary Neuron Architecture:** The `NBHGELinkPredictor`
  class implements dynamic boundary transformations through
  its `boundary_neurons` module dictionary. Each region pair
  (i,j) gets a dedicated neural network that transforms source
  node embeddings when crossing between regions i and j.

- **Region-Specific Embeddings:** Node representations are
  stored in the `node_embeds` ModuleList, enabling separate embedding tables per region while maintaining parameter efficiency through dimension sharing.

- **Composite Scoring:** The `scoring_net` combines source
  embeddings, destination embeddings, and boundary-transformed
  features to compute link probabilities, capturing both local
  and cross-region signals.

- **Adaptive Negative Sampling:** The
  `region_aware_negative_sample` function generates hard negative examples focusing on cross-region pairs, improving model
  discrimination at boundary interfaces.

- **Boundary-Aware Loss:** Training uses a balanced contrastive
  loss that separately optimizes positive and negative sample
  scores, with emphasis on boundary edges through the
  `boundary_mask` detection.

- **Dynamic Message Routing:** The forward pass automatically routes intra-region pairs through direct embeddings and
  inter-region pairs through boundary transformations, enabled
  by the region assignment tensor.

- **Scale Efficiency:** Modular region partitioning allows distributed training by processing each subgraph independently
  before boundary mediation, enabling application to massive
  graphs.

Chapter 5

Entity Resolution in Heterogeneous Graphs

This chapter presents a neural approach for entity resolution in heterogeneous datasets using the Neuron-Boundary Heterogeneous Graph Engine (NBHGE). Our implementation creates specialized boundary neurons that mediate information flow between dataset partitions (regions), enabling efficient cross-region entity comparison while preserving regional specificity. The system combines feature fusion, adaptive gating, and multi-view attention to resolve entities across diverse data modalities.

Key implementation steps:

- Partition input graph into regions based on entity types or data sources

- Initialize boundary neurons for each region containing:

  - Structural features: Graph attention over regional neighbors

  - Semantic features: Text embeddings with transformer processing

  - Numerical features: Multi-layer perceptron for tabular data

- Implement cross-region gating using boundary neuron compatibility scores

- Train through three-phase procedure:

- Regional embedding stabilization
- Boundary neuron alignment
- Resolution classifier fine-tuning

• Merge entities using adaptive similarity thresholds

Python Code Snippet

```python
import torch
import torch.nn as nn
import torch.nn.functional as F
import torch.optim as optim
from torch.nn.utils.rnn import pad_sequence
from torch_geometric.data import Data
from torch_geometric.nn import GATConv
from transformers import AutoModel, AutoTokenizer
from sklearn.metrics import f1_score
import numpy as np


# -------------------------------------------------------------
# Neuron-Boundary Heterogeneous Graph Engine (NBHGE)
# -------------------------------------------------------------
class BoundaryNeuronLayer(nn.Module):
    """
    Processes cross-region entity comparisons using multi-modal
    ↪ features:
    - Textual: Transformer-based semantic embeddings
    - Numerical: MLP-processed tabular features
    - Structural: Graph attention network outputs
    """
    def __init__(self, text_dim, num_dim, struct_dim, hidden_dim):
        super().__init__()

        # Text feature processor
        self.text_proj = nn.Sequential(
            nn.Linear(text_dim, hidden_dim),
            nn.LayerNorm(hidden_dim)
        )

        # Numerical feature processor
        self.num_proj = nn.Sequential(
            nn.Linear(num_dim, hidden_dim),
            nn.ReLU(),
            nn.Linear(hidden_dim, hidden_dim),
            nn.LayerNorm(hidden_dim)
        )

        # Structural feature processor
        self.struct_proj = nn.Sequential(
```

```python
            GATConv(struct_dim, hidden_dim, heads=3),
            nn.Linear(3*hidden_dim, hidden_dim)
        )

        # Cross-region attention gate
        self.attention = nn.MultiheadAttention(hidden_dim, 4,
        ↪  batch_first=True)

        # Compatibility scorer
        self.scorer = nn.Sequential(
            nn.Linear(3*hidden_dim, 2*hidden_dim),
            nn.ReLU(),
            nn.Linear(2*hidden_dim, 1),
            nn.Sigmoid()
        )

    def forward(self, region1, region2, edge_index):
        """
        region1/region2: Tuple containing (text_feats, num_feats,
        ↪  struct_feats)
        edge_index: Connectivity for structural processing
        Returns: Similarity scores between boundary neurons
        """
        # Process textual features
        text1 = self.text_proj(region1[0])
        text2 = self.text_proj(region2[0])

        # Process numerical features
        num1 = self.num_proj(region1[1])
        num2 = self.num_proj(region2[1])

        # Process structural features
        struct1 = self.struct_proj[0](region1[2], edge_index)
        struct1 = self.struct_proj[1](struct1)
        struct2 = self.struct_proj[0](region2[2], edge_index)
        struct2 = self.struct_proj[1](struct2)

        # Create boundary representations
        boundary1 = torch.cat([text1, num1, struct1], dim=-1)
        boundary2 = torch.cat([text2, num2, struct2], dim=-1)

        # Cross-region attention gating
        attn_out, _ = self.attention(boundary1, boundary2,
        ↪  boundary2)

        # Calculate pairwise compatibility scores
        expanded1 = attn_out.unsqueeze(2)
        expanded2 = boundary2.unsqueeze(1)
        combined = torch.cat([expanded1, expanded2,
        ↪  expanded1*expanded2], dim=-1)
        scores = self.scorer(combined).squeeze(-1)

        return scores
```

```python
class NBHGEModel(nn.Module):
    """
    Main NBHGE architecture with region-specific processors and
    ↪   boundary mediation
    """
    def __init__(self, num_regions, text_dim, num_dim, struct_dim,
    ↪   hidden_dim):
        super().__init__()

        # Region-specific initializers
        self.region_encoders = nn.ModuleList([
            nn.Linear(text_dim + num_dim + struct_dim, hidden_dim)
            for _ in range(num_regions)
        ])

        # Shared boundary processors
        self.boundary_layers = nn.ModuleList([
            BoundaryNeuronLayer(text_dim, num_dim, struct_dim,
            ↪   hidden_dim)
            for _ in range(num_regions*(num_regions-1)//2)
        ])

        # Resolution classifier
        self.classifier = nn.Sequential(
            nn.Linear(hidden_dim*3, hidden_dim),
            nn.ReLU(),
            nn.Dropout(0.3),
            nn.Linear(hidden_dim, 2)
        )

        # Feature normalizers
        self.text_norm = nn.LayerNorm(text_dim)
        self.num_norm = nn.LayerNorm(num_dim)

    def forward(self, regions, edge_indices):
        """
        regions: List of tuples (text_feats, num_feats,
        ↪   struct_feats) per region
        edge_indices: List of connectivity graphs for structural
        ↪   processing
        Returns: Resolution probabilities and boundary scores
        """
        # Normalize input features
        regions = [(self.text_norm(t), self.num_norm(n), s)
                   for t, n, s in regions]

        # Encode regional features
        encoded_regions = []
        for i, region in enumerate(regions):
            combined = torch.cat(region, dim=-1)
            encoded = self.region_encoders[i](combined)
            encoded_regions.append(encoded)
```

```python
        # Calculate boundary scores between region pairs
        boundary_scores = []
        layer_idx = 0
        for i in range(len(regions)):
            for j in range(i+1, len(regions)):
                scores = self.boundary_layers[layer_idx](
                    regions[i], regions[j], edge_indices[layer_idx]
                )
                boundary_scores.append(scores)
                layer_idx += 1

        # Create resolution features
        resolution_feats = []
        for i, enc in enumerate(encoded_regions):
            neighbors = [enc]
            for j, other_enc in enumerate(encoded_regions):
                if i != j:
                    neighbors.append(other_enc)
            combined = torch.cat(neighbors[:3], dim=-1)  # Take
            ↪ first two neighbors
            resolution_feats.append(combined)

        # Final classification
        logits = self.classifier(torch.cat(resolution_feats, dim=0))
        return F.softmax(logits, dim=-1), boundary_scores


# ----------------------------------------------------------------
# Data Handling
# ----------------------------------------------------------------
class HeteroGraphDataset:
    """Manages regions with heterogeneous node features"""
    def __init__(self, regions, edges):
        """
        regions: List of tuples (text_feats, num_feats,
        ↪ struct_feats)
        edges: List of edge_index tensors for structural processing
        """
        self.regions = regions
        self.edges = edges

    def __len__(self):
        return len(self.regions[0][0])  # Assumes equal nodes per
        ↪ region

    def get_batch(self, batch_size):
        """Sample nodes across regions maintaining alignment"""
        indices = torch.randperm(len(self))[:batch_size]
        return [
            (r[0][indices], r[1][indices], r[2][indices])
            for r in self.regions
        ], [e[:, indices] for e in self.edges]
```

38

```python
def collate_hetero_data(batch):
    """Pad variable-length features across regions"""
    padded_regions = []
    max_len = max([r[0].size(0) for region in batch for r in
    ↪   region])

    for region in zip(*batch):
        padded_text = pad_sequence([r[0] for r in region],
        ↪   batch_first=True)
        padded_num = pad_sequence([r[1] for r in region],
        ↪   batch_first=True)
        padded_struct = pad_sequence([r[2] for r in region],
        ↪   batch_first=True)
        padded_regions.append((padded_text, padded_num,
        ↪   padded_struct))

    return padded_regions

# -------------------------------------------------------------
# Training Framework
# -------------------------------------------------------------
def train_boundary_stage(model, dataset, optimizer, epochs=10):
    """Phase 1: Boundary neuron alignment"""
    model.train()
    for epoch in range(epochs):
        optimizer.zero_grad()
        regions, edges = dataset.get_batch(256)
        _, boundary_scores = model(regions, edges)

        # Contrastive loss for boundary alignment
        loss = 0
        for scores in boundary_scores:
            pos_pairs = scores.diag().mean()
            neg_pairs = (scores.sum() - scores.diag().sum()) /
            ↪   (scores.size(0)-1)
            loss += F.mse_loss(pos_pairs,
            ↪   torch.ones_like(pos_pairs)) + \
                    F.mse_loss(neg_pairs,
                    ↪   torch.zeros_like(neg_pairs))

        loss.backward()
        optimizer.step()
        print(f"Boundary Stage Epoch {epoch+1} | Loss:
        ↪   {loss.item():.4f}")

def train_resolution_stage(model, dataset, optimizer, epochs=15):
    """Phase 2: End-to-end resolution fine-tuning"""
    model.train()
    for epoch in range(epochs):
        regions, edges = dataset.get_batch(256)
        probs, _ = model(regions, edges)

        # Sample positive/negative pairs (mock implementation)
```

```
        targets = torch.cat([
            torch.ones(128),    # Assume 50% matches
            torch.zeros(128)
        ]).long()

        loss = F.cross_entropy(probs, targets)
        optimizer.zero_grad()
        loss.backward()
        optimizer.step()
        print(f"Resolution Stage Epoch {epoch+1} | Loss:
        ↪    {loss.item():.4f}")

# -------------------------------------------------------------
# Main Execution
# -------------------------------------------------------------
def main():
    # Configuration
    NUM_REGIONS = 2
    TEXT_DIM = 768   # BERT-base dimension
    NUM_DIM = 10
    STRUCT_DIM = 64

    # Mock dataset with two regions
    region1 = (
        torch.randn(1000, TEXT_DIM),   # 1000 nodes
        torch.randn(1000, NUM_DIM),
        torch.randn(1000, STRUCT_DIM)
    )
    region2 = (
        torch.randn(1000, TEXT_DIM),
        torch.randn(1000, NUM_DIM),
        torch.randn(1000, STRUCT_DIM)
    )
    edges = [torch.randint(0, 1000, (2, 2000)) for _ in
    ↪    range(NUM_REGIONS)]

    dataset = HeteroGraphDataset([region1, region2], edges)

    # Initialize model
    model = NBHGEModel(
        num_regions=NUM_REGIONS,
        text_dim=TEXT_DIM,
        num_dim=NUM_DIM,
        struct_dim=STRUCT_DIM,
        hidden_dim=256
    )

    # Multi-stage training
    boundary_optim = optim.AdamW(model.boundary_layers.parameters(),
    ↪    lr=1e-4)
    train_boundary_stage(model, dataset, boundary_optim)

    resolution_optim = optim.AdamW(model.parameters(), lr=5e-5)
```

```
    train_resolution_stage(model, dataset, resolution_optim)

    # Evaluation (mock implementation)
    test_regions, test_edges = dataset.get_batch(500)
    with torch.no_grad():
        probs, _ = model(test_regions, test_edges)
    preds = probs.argmax(dim=-1)
    print(f"F1 Score: {f1_score(preds.numpy(),
    ↪ np.random.randint(0,2,500)):.4f}")

if __name__ == "__main__":
    main()
```

Key Implementation Details:

- **Boundary Neuron Architecture:** The `BoundaryNeuronLayer` integrates three feature processors: transformer-based text projection (`text_proj`), MLP-based numerical processing (`num_proj`), and graph attention structural analysis (`struct_proj`). These components create unified boundary representations for cross-region comparison.

- **Multi-Head Attention Gating:** The `attention` layer in boundary neurons mediates information flow between regions using multi-head attention over fused boundary representations, enabling adaptive focus on relevant cross-region features.

- **Three-Phase Training:** The system first stabilizes boundary neuron alignment with contrastive loss (`train_boundary_stage`), then fine-tunes the entire model for resolution tasks (`train_resolution_stage`), ensuring proper feature learning hierarchy.

- **Heterogeneous Feature Fusion:** The `NBHGEModel` explicitly handles different data modalities through separate normalization paths (`text_norm`, `num_norm`) before combining them in region-specific encoders.

- **Adaptive Resolution Scoring:** The compatibility scorer in `BoundaryNeuronLayer` uses concatenated interaction features (element-wise product and original vectors) to capture complex matching patterns between entities.

- **Structural Awareness:** Graph attention convolution (`GATConv`) in boundary processing incorporates neighborhood topology, allowing the model to consider both node features and graph structure during resolution decisions.

Chapter 6

Recommendation Systems with Boundary-Based Collaborative Filtering

This chapter presents a neural recommendation framework using Neuron-Boundary Heterogeneous Graph Engines (NBHGE) that partitions users and items into semantic regions connected through learned boundary neurons. The system dynamically routes interaction signals through specialized boundary units that mediate cross-region preferences while maintaining regional specialization.

Key implementation components:

- **Region Partitioning:** Assign users/items to specialized regions using metadata or clustering

- **Boundary Neuron Initialization:** Create trainable boundary units between each region pair

- **Heterogeneous Message Passing:**

  - Intra-region aggregation using standard graph convolution

  - Cross-region communication through boundary neurons

  - Dynamic attention routing for boundary signal selection

- **Cold-Start Handling:** Special boundary neurons dedicated to new items/users

- **Training Protocol:** Bayesian Personalized Ranking (BPR) loss with boundary regularization

Python Code Snippet

```python
import torch
import torch.nn as nn
import torch.nn.functional as F
from torch.utils.data import Dataset, DataLoader
from torch.nn.utils.rnn import pad_sequence
import numpy as np
from collections import defaultdict

# -----------------------------------------------------------
# Neuron-Boundary Heterogeneous Graph Engine (Core Implementation)
# -----------------------------------------------------------
class NBHGE(nn.Module):
    """
    Neural recommendation system with boundary-mediated cross-region
    ↪   messaging
    Architecture Components:
    - User/item region assignments (pre-computed or learned)
    - Per-region embedding tables
    - Trainable boundary neurons between region pairs
    - Multi-hop message passing with boundary gates
    """
    def __init__(self, num_users, num_items, num_regions,
                 embed_dim=64, boundary_dim=None, num_layers=3):
        super().__init__()
        self.num_regions = num_regions
        self.embed_dim = embed_dim
        self.boundary_dim = boundary_dim if boundary_dim is not None
        ↪   else embed_dim
        self.num_layers = num_layers

        # Region-aware embeddings
        self.user_embeddings = nn.ModuleList([
            nn.Embedding(num_users, embed_dim) for _ in
            ↪   range(num_regions)
        ])
        self.item_embeddings = nn.ModuleList([
            nn.Embedding(num_items, embed_dim) for _ in
            ↪   range(num_regions)
        ])

        # Boundary neurons and transformation matrices
        self.boundaries = nn.ParameterDict({
```

```python
            f'{i}-{j}': nn.Parameter(torch.randn(self.boundary_dim,
            ↪   embed_dim))
            for i in range(num_regions)
            for j in range(num_regions)
            if i != j
        })

        # Message projection networks
        self.msg_proj = nn.Sequential(
            nn.Linear(2*embed_dim, self.boundary_dim),
            nn.LeakyReLU(0.2)
        )

        # Region assignment maps (pretrained or learned)
        self.register_buffer('user_regions', torch.randint(0,
        ↪   num_regions, (num_users,)))
        self.register_buffer('item_regions', torch.randint(0,
        ↪   num_regions, (num_items,)))

        # Cold-start boundary (special region -1)
        self.cs_boundary = nn.Parameter(torch.randn(embed_dim,
        ↪   embed_dim))

        # Layer normalization and dropout
        self.norm = nn.LayerNorm(embed_dim)
        self.dropout = nn.Dropout(0.2)

    def forward(self, user_ids, item_ids):
        """
        Forward pass with boundary-mediated message propagation
        1. Retrieve base embeddings from assigned regions
        2. Aggregate intra-region context
        3. Propagate cross-region signals through boundaries
        4. Combine representations across hops
        """
        # Get initial regional embeddings
        user_emb = self._get_regional_embeddings(user_ids,
        ↪   is_user=True)
        item_emb = self._get_regional_embeddings(item_ids,
        ↪   is_user=False)

        # Multi-hop message passing
        for _ in range(self.num_layers):
            # Intra-region aggregation
            user_emb = self.norm(user_emb +
            ↪   self._intra_region_update(user_ids, is_user=True))
            item_emb = self.norm(item_emb +
            ↪   self._intra_region_update(item_ids, is_user=False))

            # Cross-region boundary propagation
            user_emb = self._boundary_update(user_emb, user_ids,
            ↪   is_user=True)
```

```python
        item_emb = self._boundary_update(item_emb, item_ids,
            is_user=False)

        # Final prediction scores
        return torch.matmul(user_emb, item_emb.T)

    def _get_regional_embeddings(self, ids, is_user):
        """Retrieve region-specific embeddings with cold-start
            fallback"""
        regions = self.user_regions[ids] if is_user else
            self.item_regions[ids]
        emb_table = self.user_embeddings if is_user else
            self.item_embeddings

        # Handle cold-start items (region=-1)
        mask = (regions == -1)
        if mask.any():
            base_emb = torch.stack([
                emb_table[regions[i]](ids[i]) if not mask[i]
                else torch.zeros(self.embed_dim,
                    device=self.cs_boundary.device)
                for i in range(len(ids))])

                # Apply cold-start boundary transformation
                base_emb[mask] = torch.matmul(
                    base_emb[mask], self.cs_boundary
                )
        else:
            base_emb = torch.stack([emb_table[r](id)
                                    for r, id in zip(regions, ids)])

        return base_emb

    def _intra_region_update(self, ids, is_user):
        """Aggregate messages from same-region neighbors"""
        # Simplified example - real implementation uses adjacency
            lists
        return self.dropout(
            torch.randn(len(ids), self.embed_dim,
                device=self.cs_boundary.device) * 0.1  # Mock
                neighborhood aggregation
        )

    def _boundary_update(self, embeddings, ids, is_user):
        """Propagate embeddings through boundary neurons"""
        regions = self.user_regions[ids] if is_user else
            self.item_regions[ids]
        updated = embeddings.clone()

        for i, r in enumerate(regions):
            # Get all boundaries for current region
            for boundary_key in self.boundaries:
                src_reg, dst_reg = map(int, boundary_key.split('-'))
```

46

```python
                if r == src_reg:
                    # Transform embedding through boundary
                    boundary_matrix = self.boundaries[boundary_key]
                    transformed = F.leaky_relu(
                        torch.matmul(embeddings[i],
                        ↪   boundary_matrix.T)
                    )
                    # Gate boundary signal
                    gate = torch.sigmoid(
                        torch.mean(transformed) * 0.5  # Simplified
                        ↪   gating
                    )
                    updated[i] += gate * transformed

        return self.norm(updated)


# ------------------------------------------------------------------
# Dataset and DataLoader
# ------------------------------------------------------------------
class RecDataset(Dataset):
    """User-item interaction dataset with region metadata"""
    def __init__(self, interactions, num_users, num_items):
        self.user_items = defaultdict(list)
        for u, i, r in interactions:
            self.user_items[u].append((i, r))
        self.num_users = num_users
        self.num_items = num_items

    def __len__(self):
        return self.num_users

    def __getitem__(self, user_id):
        pos_items = [i for i, _ in self.user_items[user_id]]
        return {
            'user': user_id,
            'pos_items': torch.LongTensor(pos_items),
            'neg_items': torch.LongTensor(np.random.choice(
                self.num_items, len(pos_items), replace=False
            ))
        }


def collate_fn(batch):
    """Custom collate for variable-length user interactions"""
    return {
        'users': torch.LongTensor([x['user'] for x in batch]),
        'pos_items': pad_sequence(
            [x['pos_items'] for x in batch], batch_first=True
        ),
        'neg_items': pad_sequence(
            [x['neg_items'] for x in batch], batch_first=True
        )
    }
```

```python
# -----------------------------------------------------------
# Training and Evaluation
# -----------------------------------------------------------
def train_epoch(model, dataloader, optimizer, device):
    model.train()
    total_loss = 0
    for batch in dataloader:
        users = batch['users'].to(device)
        pos_items = batch['pos_items'].to(device)
        neg_items = batch['neg_items'].to(device)

        optimizer.zero_grad()

        # Get user and item embeddings
        user_emb = model._get_regional_embeddings(users,
        ↪   is_user=True)
        pos_emb = model._get_regional_embeddings(pos_items,
        ↪   is_user=False)
        neg_emb = model._get_regional_embeddings(neg_items,
        ↪   is_user=False)

        # Calculate BPR loss
        pos_scores = torch.sum(user_emb.unsqueeze(1) * pos_emb,
        ↪   dim=-1)
        neg_scores = torch.sum(user_emb.unsqueeze(1) * neg_emb,
        ↪   dim=-1)
        loss = -torch.mean(F.logsigmoid(pos_scores - neg_scores))

        # Boundary regularization
        boundary_reg = sum(
            torch.norm(b, p=2) for b in model.boundaries.values()
        ) * 0.01
        loss += boundary_reg

        loss.backward()
        optimizer.step()
        total_loss += loss.item() * len(users)
    return total_loss / len(dataloader.dataset)


# -----------------------------------------------------------
# Main Execution
# -----------------------------------------------------------
def main():
    # Configuration
    NUM_USERS = 1000
    NUM_ITEMS = 5000
    NUM_REGIONS = 5
    BATCH_SIZE = 32

    # Sample interactions (user_id, item_id, rating)
    train_data = [
        (0, 100, 5), (0, 201, 4), (1, 150, 3),
        (2, 300, 5), (3, 201, 4), (4, 450, 5)
```

```
]

# Initialize components
device = torch.device('cuda' if torch.cuda.is_available() else
↪  'cpu')
dataset = RecDataset(train_data, NUM_USERS, NUM_ITEMS)
dataloader = DataLoader(
    dataset, batch_size=BATCH_SIZE, collate_fn=collate_fn,
    ↪  shuffle=True
)

model = NBHGE(
    num_users=NUM_USERS,
    num_items=NUM_ITEMS,
    num_regions=NUM_REGIONS,
    embed_dim=64
).to(device)

optimizer = torch.optim.Adam(model.parameters(), lr=0.001)

# Training loop
for epoch in range(1, 11):
    loss = train_epoch(model, dataloader, optimizer, device)
    print(f"Epoch {epoch} | Loss: {loss:.4f}")

if __name__ == "__main__":
    main()
```

Key Implementation Details:

- **Region-Boundary Architecture:** The `NBHGE` class implements region-specific embedding tables and boundary neuron matrices. Each `user_embeddings` and `item_embeddings`
  contains separate embedding layers per region.

- **Dynamic Boundary Routing:** The `_boundary_update`
  method routes embeddings through relevant boundary neurons using learned transformation matrices and gating mechanisms, enabling controlled cross-region communication.

- **Cold-Start Handling:** Special treatment for items/users
  with region=-1 in `_get_regional_embeddings` applies the
  `cs_boundary` transformation to initialize cold-start entities.

- **Heterogeneous Message Passing:** The forward pass al-
  ternates between intra-region aggregation (`_intra_region_update`)
  and cross-region propagation (`_boundary_update`) over multiple hops.

49

- **Regularized Training:** The BPR loss in `train_epoch` includes L2 regularization on boundary neuron parameters to prevent overfitting during cross-region signal exchange.

- **Region-Aware Sampling:** The `RecDataset` class organizes interactions while preserving regional membership information needed for boundary routing decisions.

Chapter 7

Anomaly Detection via Multi-Region Graph Partitioning

This chapter implements the Neuron-Boundary Heterogeneous Graph Engine (NBHGE) for identifying anomalies through adaptive graph partitioning and boundary neuron analysis. The system dynamically divides heterogeneous graphs into semantically coherent regions connected via specialized boundary nodes that monitor inter-region interactions. By comparing intra-region patterns with cross-partition signals, the model detects nodes exhibiting abnormal connectivity patterns.

Key implementation steps:

- Initialize heterogeneous graph with node features and edge connections

- Learn region assignments through trainable feature projections

- Identify boundary nodes through inter-region edge analysis

- Process region-specific features with dedicated transformation networks

- Compute cross-region context via multi-head boundary attention

- Calculate anomaly scores as divergence between local and boundary features

- Optimize region partitions through backpropagation of anomaly signals

Python Code Snippet

```python
import torch
import torch.nn as nn
import torch.nn.functional as F
import torch.optim as optim
from torch.utils.data import Dataset, DataLoader
import numpy as np
from sklearn.metrics import roc_auc_score

# ----------------------------------------------------------
# Neuron-Boundary Heterogeneous Graph Engine (NBHGE)
# ----------------------------------------------------------
class NBHGE(nn.Module):
    """
    Implements multi-region anomaly detection through:
    1. Adaptive graph partitioning
    2. Boundary-mediated cross-region attention
    3. Divergence-based anomaly scoring

    Architecture Components:
    - region_assigner: Learns optimal node-to-region mappings
    - region_mlps: Region-specific feature processors
    - boundary_attns: Cross-region attention mediators
    - score_net: Computes node-boundary divergence scores
    """
    def __init__(self, num_regions, input_dim, hidden_dim,
    ↪  num_heads):
        super().__init__()
        self.num_regions = num_regions

        # Region assignment layer (softmax over region logits)
        self.region_assigner = nn.Linear(input_dim, num_regions)

        # Region-specific feature processors
        self.region_mlps = nn.ModuleList([
            nn.Sequential(
                nn.Linear(input_dim, hidden_dim),
                nn.ReLU(),
                nn.LayerNorm(hidden_dim)
            ) for _ in range(num_regions)
        ])

        # Boundary attention modules (one per region)
```

```python
        self.boundary_attns = nn.ModuleList([
            nn.MultiheadAttention(hidden_dim, num_heads)
            for _ in range(num_regions)
        ])

        # Anomaly scoring network
        self.score_net = nn.Sequential(
            nn.Linear(hidden_dim * 2, hidden_dim),
            nn.ReLU(),
            nn.Linear(hidden_dim, 1),
            nn.Sigmoid()
        )

    def forward(self, x, edge_index):
        """
        x: Node features [num_nodes, input_dim]
        edge_index: Edge connections [2, num_edges]
        Returns: Anomaly probabilities [num_nodes]
        """
        # Region Assignment (learnable partitioning)
        region_probs = F.softmax(self.region_assigner(x), dim=1)
        region_assign = region_probs.argmax(dim=1)

        # Region-Specific Feature Processing (differentiable)
        node_embeddings = torch.zeros(x.size(0),
        ↪   self.region_mlps[0][0].out_features, device=x.device)
        for region_idx in range(self.num_regions):
            region_features = self.region_mlps[region_idx](x)
            node_embeddings += region_probs[:,
            ↪   region_idx].unsqueeze(1) * region_features

        # Boundary Node Identification (detached)
        with torch.no_grad():
            src, dst = edge_index
            cross_region_mask = (region_assign[src] !=
            ↪   region_assign[dst])
            boundary_nodes =
            ↪   torch.unique(torch.cat([src[cross_region_mask],
            ↪   dst[cross_region_mask]]))

        # Cross-Region Context Aggregation
        boundary_contexts = torch.zeros_like(node_embeddings)
        for node in boundary_nodes:
            region_idx = region_assign[node].item()
            other_regions_mask = (region_assign != region_idx)
            other_embs = node_embeddings[other_regions_mask]

            if other_embs.size(0) > 0:
                query =
                ↪   node_embeddings[node].unsqueeze(0).unsqueeze(0)
                key = value = other_embs.unsqueeze(0)
```

```python
        attn_output, _ =
        ↪ self.boundary_attns[region_idx](query, key,
        ↪ value)
        boundary_contexts[node] = attn_output.squeeze(0)

    # Anomaly Score Calculation
    combined_features = torch.cat([node_embeddings,
    ↪ boundary_contexts], dim=1)
    return self.score_net(combined_features).squeeze(1)


# ---------------------------------------------------------
# Graph Dataset and Data Loading
# ---------------------------------------------------------
class GraphDataset(Dataset):
    """Custom dataset for graph anomaly detection"""
    def __init__(self, node_features, edge_indices, labels):
        self.node_features = node_features   # List of feature
        ↪ tensors
        self.edge_indices = edge_indices      # List of edge index
        ↪ tensors
        self.labels = labels                  # List of label tensors

    def __len__(self):
        return len(self.node_features)

    def __getitem__(self, idx):
        return (
            self.node_features[idx],
            self.edge_indices[idx],
            self.labels[idx]
        )


# ---------------------------------------------------------
# Training and Evaluation Functions
# ---------------------------------------------------------
def train_epoch(model, dataloader, optimizer, device):
    model.train()
    total_loss = 0.0
    total_nodes = 0
    for x, edge_index, labels in dataloader:
        x, edge_index, labels = x.to(device), edge_index.to(device),
        ↪ labels.to(device)
        optimizer.zero_grad()
        scores = model(x, edge_index)
        loss = F.binary_cross_entropy(scores, labels.float())
        loss.backward()
        optimizer.step()
        total_loss += loss.item() * x.size(0)
        total_nodes += x.size(0)
    return total_loss / total_nodes if total_nodes > 0 else 0.0

def evaluate(model, dataloader, device):
    model.eval()
```

```python
    all_scores, all_labels = [], []
    with torch.no_grad():
        for x, edge_index, labels in dataloader:
            x, edge_index = x.to(device), edge_index.to(device)
            scores = model(x, edge_index)
            all_scores.extend(scores.cpu().numpy())
            all_labels.extend(labels.cpu().numpy())
    return roc_auc_score(all_labels, all_scores)


# ----------------------------------------------------------------
# Main Execution
# ----------------------------------------------------------------
def main():
    # Configuration
    num_nodes = 1000
    input_dim = 64
    num_regions = 4

    # Synthetic data generation
    node_features = [torch.randn(num_nodes, input_dim)]
    edge_indices = [torch.randint(0, num_nodes, (2, 5000),
    ↪   dtype=torch.long)]
    labels = [torch.randint(0, 2, (num_nodes,))]

    # Initialize dataset and dataloader
    dataset = GraphDataset(node_features, edge_indices, labels)
    dataloader = DataLoader(dataset, batch_size=1, shuffle=True)

    # Model setup
    device = torch.device('cuda' if torch.cuda.is_available() else
    ↪   'cpu')
    model = NBHGE(
        num_regions=num_regions,
        input_dim=input_dim,
        hidden_dim=128,
        num_heads=4
    ).to(device)
    optimizer = optim.Adam(model.parameters(), lr=0.001)

    # Training loop
    for epoch in range(1, 6):
        loss = train_epoch(model, dataloader, optimizer, device)
        auc = evaluate(model, dataloader, device)
        print(f"Epoch {epoch} | Loss: {loss:.4f} | AUC: {auc:.4f}")


if __name__ == "__main__":
    main()
```

Key Implementation Details:

- **Adaptive Region Partitioning:** The `region_assigner` layer learns optimal node-to-region mappings through end-to-end training, enabling dynamic graph partitioning based on feature similarity and connectivity patterns.

- **Boundary Attention Mechanism:** Each region maintains dedicated `boundary_attns` modules that compute context vectors through multi-head attention over adjacent regions' nodes, effectively highlighting cross-partition discrepancies.

- **Divergence Scoring:** The `score_net` combines local region embeddings with boundary contexts using a non-linear transformation, producing anomaly probabilities through sigmoid activation.

- **Edge-Aware Boundary Detection:** Boundary nodes are automatically identified through analysis of inter-region edges in `edge_index`, focusing computation on critical partition-crossing connections.

- **Region-Specialized Processing:** Separate `region_mlps` allow customized feature transformation for each subgraph while maintaining parameter efficiency through component modularity.

- **Stabilized Training:** Layer normalization in region processors and softmax-based region assignment prevent gradient instability during joint partition learning and boundary optimization.

Chapter 8

Dimensionality Reduction with Multi-Level Graph Embeddings

This chapter presents a neural framework for graph dimensionality reduction through hierarchical region partitioning and boundary mediation. Our Neuron-Boundary Heterogeneous Graph Engine (NBHGE) decomposes large graphs into specialized sub-regions connected via learned boundary neurons that coordinate inter-region relationships while preserving local topology.

Key implementation strategy:

- **Graph Decomposition:**

    - Partition input graph into orthogonal regions using spectral clustering

    - Identify boundary nodes connecting adjacent subgraphs

- **Boundary Neuron Setup:**

    - Initialize trainable boundary embeddings between regions

    - Establish gating mechanisms for cross-region communication

- **Multi-Level Processing:**
  - First reduce dimensions within individual regions
  - Align regional embeddings through boundary mediators
  - Apply iterative refinement across resolution levels

- **Optimization Objectives:**
  - Preserve local neighborhood relationships within regions
  - Maintain consistent boundary representations across regions
  - Minimize reconstruction error across resolution levels

Python Code Snippet

```python
import torch
import torch.nn as nn
import torch.nn.functional as F
import numpy as np
from sklearn.manifold import TSNE
from torch_geometric.utils import to_dense_adj, dense_to_sparse

# -------------------------------------------------------------
# Neuron-Boundary Heterogeneous Graph Engine (NBHGE)
# -------------------------------------------------------------
class NBHGEngine(nn.Module):
    """
    Hierarchical dimensionality reduction with:
    - Region-specific embedding networks
    - Trainable boundary neurons between partitions
    - Multi-level alignment constraints
    """
    def __init__(self, input_dim, hidden_dims, output_dim,
    ↪ num_regions,
                 boundary_size=32, dropout=0.2):
        super().__init__()
        self.num_regions = num_regions
        self.boundary_size = boundary_size

        # Region embedding networks
        self.region_encoders = nn.ModuleList([
            nn.Sequential(
                nn.Linear(input_dim, hidden_dims[0]),
                nn.ReLU(),
                nn.Dropout(dropout)
            ) for _ in range(num_regions)
        ])
```

```python
        # Boundary gating network
        self.boundary_mediator = nn.Sequential(
            nn.Linear(2*hidden_dims[0], boundary_size),
            nn.Tanh(),
            nn.Linear(boundary_size, hidden_dims[0]),
            nn.Sigmoid()
        )

        # Multi-level projection
        self.projection = nn.Sequential(
            nn.Linear(hidden_dims[0]*num_regions, hidden_dims[1]),
            nn.ELU(),
            nn.Linear(hidden_dims[1], output_dim),
            nn.LayerNorm(output_dim)
        )

        # Boundary alignment parameters
        self.boundary_align = nn.Parameter(
            torch.randn(num_regions, num_regions, hidden_dims[0])
        )

    def forward(self, x, adj, regions):
        """
        x: Node features [N, input_dim]
        adj: Full adjacency matrix [N, N]
        regions: Region assignments [N]
        """
        # Partition graph into regions
        regional_embeddings = []
        boundary_maps = {}

        # Phase 1: Intra-region embedding
        for i in range(self.num_regions):
            mask = (regions == i)
            regional_x = x[mask]
            enc = self.region_encoders[i](regional_x)
            regional_embeddings.append(enc)

            # Identify boundary nodes (connected to other regions)
            adj_i = adj[mask]
            external_connections = adj_i[:, ~mask].sum(1) > 0
            boundary_nodes = enc[external_connections]
            boundary_maps[i] = boundary_nodes

        # Phase 2: Boundary mediation
        aligned_embeddings = []
        for i in range(self.num_regions):
            main_emb = regional_embeddings[i]

            # Collect boundary context from adjacent regions
            boundary_context = []
            for j in range(self.num_regions):
```

```
                if i == j: continue
                if j not in boundary_maps: continue

                # Calculate boundary alignment scores
                align_weights = torch.matmul(
                    main_emb,
                    self.boundary_align[i,j]
                )
                mediated = self.boundary_mediator(
                    torch.cat([main_emb.mean(0),
                    ↪   boundary_maps[j].mean(0)])
                )
                boundary_context.append(mediated * align_weights)

            # Combine regional and boundary information
            boundary_sum = torch.stack(boundary_context).sum(0) if
            ↪   boundary_context else 0
            aligned = main_emb + boundary_sum
            aligned_embeddings.append(aligned)

        # Phase 3: Multi-level projection
        concatenated = torch.cat([
            emb.mean(0) for emb in aligned_embeddings
        ])
        final_embedding = self.projection(concatenated)

        return final_embedding


# ------------------------------------------------------------
# Graph Processing Functions
# ------------------------------------------------------------
def create_graph_data(num_nodes=512, feat_dim=1024):
    """Generate synthetic graph with community structure"""
    adj_probs = torch.eye(num_nodes)*0.8 +
    ↪   torch.rand(num_nodes,num_nodes)*0.2
    adj_probs = torch.clamp(adj_probs, 0.0, 1.0)
    adj = torch.bernoulli(adj_probs)
    features = torch.randn(num_nodes, feat_dim)
    regions = torch.randint(0, 4, (num_nodes,))
    return adj, features, regions

def adjacency_reconstruction_loss(embedding, original_adj):
    """Preserve topological relationships in latent space"""
    reconstructed = torch.sigmoid(torch.mm(embedding,
    ↪   embedding.t()))
    return F.mse_loss(reconstructed, original_adj)


# ------------------------------------------------------------
# Training and Evaluation
# ------------------------------------------------------------
def train_nbhge(model, optimizer, epochs=100):
    adj, features, regions = create_graph_data()
    model.train()
```

```python
    for epoch in range(epochs):
        optimizer.zero_grad()
        embedding = model(features, adj, regions)

        # Multi-objective loss components
        recon_loss = adjacency_reconstruction_loss(embedding, adj)
        boundary_loss = torch.norm(model.boundary_align) * 0.1   #
        ↪  Regularization
        manifold_loss = -torch.cov(embedding.t()).trace() * 0.01   #
        ↪  Diversity

        total_loss = recon_loss + boundary_loss + manifold_loss
        total_loss.backward()
        optimizer.step()

        if epoch % 10 == 0:
            print(f"Epoch {epoch} | Loss: {total_loss.item():.4f}")

def visualize_embeddings(embedding):
    """Project final embeddings to 2D for visualization"""
    tsne = TSNE(n_components=2)
    vis =
    ↪  tsne.fit_transform(embedding.unsqueeze(0).detach().numpy())
    plt.scatter(vis[:,0], vis[:,1])
    plt.title("NBHGE Dimensionality Reduction")
    plt.show()

# ------------------------------------------------------------
# Main Execution
# ------------------------------------------------------------
if __name__ == "__main__":
    # Initialize NBHGE model
    nbhge = NBHGEngine(
        input_dim=1024,
        hidden_dims=[256, 64],
        output_dim=32,
        num_regions=4,
        boundary_size=64
    )

    # Set up optimization
    optimizer = torch.optim.AdamW(nbhge.parameters(), lr=0.001)

    # Train the model
    train_nbhge(nbhge, optimizer, epochs=50)

    # Generate final embeddings
    adj, features, regions = create_graph_data()
    with torch.no_grad():
        final_emb = nbhge(features, adj, regions)

    # Visualization
```

Key Implementation Details:

- **Boundary Neuron Mechanics:** The `boundary_mediator` network processes cross-region information flow through learnable alignment parameters (`boundary_align`), using both additive and multiplicative interactions to preserve topological relationships.

- **Multi-Phase Processing:**

    - *Intra-Region Encoding:* Separate MLPs process each partitioned subgraph

    - *Boundary Negotiation:* Specialized attention-like mechanisms align embeddings at region interfaces

    - *Hierarchical Projection:* Progressive dimensionality reduction through multiple fully-connected layers

- **Loss Architecture:** Combines three complementary objectives:

    - `recon_loss`: Maintains adjacency relationships in latent space

    - `boundary_loss`: Regularizes boundary neuron activations

    - `manifold_loss`: Encourages diverse, spread-out embeddings

- **Dynamic Partitioning:** While this implementation uses fixed region assignments, the architecture supports integration with learnable graph partitioning modules through gradient estimators.

- **Scale Preservation:** The `adjacency_reconstruction_loss` ensures local neighborhood structures are maintained despite dimensional reduction, critical for downstream graph tasks.

- **Adaptive Boundary Gates:** The `boundary_mediator`'s sigmoid activation allows soft information flow control between regions, learning when to permit cross-partition communication.

Chapter 9

Graph-Based Query Expansion and Information Retrieval

This chapter implements a query expansion system using the Neuron-Boundary Heterogeneous Graph Engine (NBHGE). Our architecture constructs a multimodal graph connecting search queries, documents, and terms through learned boundary neurons that control information flow between specialized subgraphs. The system dynamically expands queries by traversing relevant graph regions guided by these boundary mediators.

Key implementation steps:

- Construct heterogeneous graph with three node types:

  - **Query Nodes:** Represent user search intents with temporal metadata
  - **Document Nodes:** Contain content embeddings and retrieval statistics
  - **Term Nodes:** Store lexical information and co-occurrence patterns

- Implement boundary neurons as gating mechanisms between subgraphs

- Develop multi-phase training with alternating objectives:

  - Phase 1: Learn basic query-term expansions

- Phase 2: Incorporate document-click relationships
- Phase 3: Fine-tune with domain-specific constraints

- Fuse structural and semantic features through boundary-mediated walks

- Generate expanded queries using learned graph trajectories

Python Code Snippet

```python
import torch
import torch.nn as nn
import torch.nn.functional as F
from torch_geometric.data import HeteroData
from torch_geometric.nn import HeteroConv, GATConv, SAGEConv
from collections import defaultdict

# ------------------------------------------------------------
# Heterogeneous Graph Construction
# ------------------------------------------------------------
class GraphBuilder:
    """Builds heterogeneous graph with query/doc/term nodes and
    ↪    typed edges"""
    def __init__(self):
        self.node_store = {
            'query': [],
            'doc': [],
            'term': []
        }
        self.edge_index = {
            ('query', 'expand', 'term'): [],
            ('term', 'related', 'term'): [],
            ('doc', 'contains', 'term'): [],
            ('query', 'click', 'doc'): []
        }
        self.node_features = defaultdict(dict)

    def add_query_node(self, query_id, features):
        self.node_store['query'].append(query_id)
        self.node_features['query'][query_id] = features

    def add_doc_node(self, doc_id, features):
        self.node_store['doc'].append(doc_id)
        self.node_features['doc'][doc_id] = features

    def add_term_node(self, term, features):
        self.node_store['term'].append(term)
        self.node_features['term'][term] = features
```

```python
    def add_edge(self, src_type, relation, dest_type, src_id,
    ↪ dest_id):
        self.edge_index[(src_type, relation, dest_type)].append(
            (self._get_index(src_type, src_id),
             self._get_index(dest_type, dest_id))
        )

    def _get_index(self, node_type, node_id):
        return self.node_store[node_type].index(node_id)

    def to_pyg_data(self):
        """Convert to PyTorch Geometric HeteroData object"""
        data = HeteroData()

        # Add node features
        for node_type in self.node_store:
            node_ids = self.node_store[node_type]
            if not node_ids:
                continue
            if self.node_features[node_type]:
                feats = [self.node_features[node_type][nid] for nid
                ↪ in node_ids]
                data[node_type].x = torch.stack(feats)

        # Add edge indices
        for edge_type in self.edge_index:
            src_type, rel_type, dst_type = edge_type
            edges = self.edge_index[edge_type]
            if edges:
                edge_tensor = torch.tensor(edges).t().contiguous()
                data[edge_type].edge_index = edge_tensor

        return data


# ------------------------------------------------------------
# NBHGE Model Architecture
# ------------------------------------------------------------
class NBHGEModel(nn.Module):
    """Neuron-Boundary Heterogeneous Graph Engine"""
    def __init__(self, hidden_dim=256, boundary_dim=128,
    ↪ num_heads=4):
        super().__init__()

        # Type-specific transformation layers
        self.query_embed = nn.Linear(128, hidden_dim)   # Query
        ↪ feature dimension 128
        self.doc_embed = nn.Linear(512, hidden_dim)      # Doc feature
        ↪ dimension 512
        self.term_embed = nn.Linear(128, hidden_dim)    # Term
        ↪ feature dimension 128

        # Boundary neuron gates
        self.boundary_mlp = nn.Sequential(
```

```python
            nn.Linear(hidden_dim*2, boundary_dim),
            nn.ReLU(),
            nn.Linear(boundary_dim, 1),
            nn.Sigmoid()
        )

        # Heterogeneous convolution layers
        self.conv1 = HeteroConv({
            ('query', 'expand', 'term'): GATConv(hidden_dim,
            ↪   hidden_dim, num_heads),
            ('term', 'related', 'term'): SAGEConv(hidden_dim,
            ↪   hidden_dim),
            ('doc', 'contains', 'term'): SAGEConv(hidden_dim,
            ↪   hidden_dim),
            ('query', 'click', 'doc'): GATConv(hidden_dim,
            ↪   hidden_dim, num_heads)
        }, aggr='mean')

        self.conv2 = HeteroConv({
            ('term', 'related', 'term'): SAGEConv(hidden_dim,
            ↪   hidden_dim),
            ('doc', 'contains', 'term'): SAGEConv(hidden_dim,
            ↪   hidden_dim)
        }, aggr='max')

    def forward(self, data, target_query_ids):
        # Initialize embeddings from node features
        x_dict = {
            'query': self.query_embed(data['query'].x),
            'doc': self.doc_embed(data['doc'].x),
            'term': self.term_embed(data['term'].x)
        }

        # First heterogeneous convolution
        x_dict = self.conv1(x_dict, data.edge_index_dict)
        x_dict = {key: F.leaky_relu(x) for key, x in x_dict.items()}

        # Boundary-mediated aggregation
        expanded_queries = []
        for qid in target_query_ids:
            query_idx =
            ↪   data['query'].x[:,0].eq(qid).nonzero().item()
            query_feat = x_dict['query'][query_idx]

            # Get connected terms through 'expand' edges
            term_edges = data[('query', 'expand',
            ↪   'term')].edge_index
            connected_terms = term_edges[1][term_edges[0] ==
            ↪   query_idx]

            # Boundary gating for query expansion
            term_weights = []
            for term_idx in connected_terms:
```

```python
            term_feat = x_dict['term'][term_idx]
            boundary_input = torch.cat([query_feat, term_feat],
            ↪   dim=-1)
            gate = self.boundary_mlp(boundary_input)
            term_weights.append(gate * term_feat)

        # Aggregate weighted term features
        if term_weights:
            expanded_feat =
            ↪   torch.stack(term_weights).mean(dim=0)
        else:
            expanded_feat = torch.zeros_like(query_feat)
        x_dict['query'][query_idx] += expanded_feat

        expanded_queries.append(x_dict['query'][query_idx])

    # Second convolution on updated graph
    x_dict = self.conv2(x_dict, data.edge_index_dict)
    return torch.stack(expanded_queries)

# ------------------------------------------------------------
# Training Infrastructure
# ------------------------------------------------------------
class NBHGELoss(nn.Module):
    """Composite loss for expansion quality and retrieval
    ↪   performance"""
    def __init__(self, alpha=0.7):
        super().__init__()
        self.alpha = alpha
        self.expansion_loss = nn.CosineEmbeddingLoss()
        self.retrieval_loss = nn.CrossEntropyLoss()

    def forward(self, expanded_queries, doc_embeddings,
    ↪   target_docs):
        # Expansion similarity loss
        sim_loss = self.expansion_loss(
            expanded_queries[:-1], expanded_queries[1:],
            torch.ones(expanded_queries.size(0)-1).
            to(expanded_queries.device)
        )

        # Document retrieval loss
        scores = torch.mm(expanded_queries, doc_embeddings.t())
        ret_loss = self.retrieval_loss(scores, target_docs)

        return self.alpha * sim_loss + (1 - self.alpha) * ret_loss

def train_phase(model, data, optimizer, phase=1):
    """Multi-phase training with different edge type emphasis"""
    model.train()
    optimizer.zero_grad()

    # Phase-specific edge masking
```

```
    if phase == 1:
        edge_mask = {et: et[1] == 'expand' for et in
        ↪  data.edge_index_dict}
    elif phase == 2:
        edge_mask = {et: et[1] == 'click' for et in
        ↪  data.edge_index_dict}
    else:
        edge_mask = None

    # Forward pass with phase-specific edges
    outputs = model(data,
    ↪  target_query_ids=data['query'].x[:,0].long().tolist())

    # Compute composite loss
    loss_fn = NBHGELoss()
    loss = loss_fn(outputs, data['doc'].x,
    ↪  target_docs=data['doc'].x[:,0].long())

    loss.backward()
    optimizer.step()
    return loss.item()

# ------------------------------------------------------------
# Example Usage
# ------------------------------------------------------------
def main():
    # Build sample graph
    builder = GraphBuilder()

    # Add nodes
    builder.add_query_node(0, features=torch.randn(128))  # Query
    ↪  "AI research"
    builder.add_term_node("artificial", torch.randn(128))
    builder.add_term_node("intelligence", torch.randn(128))
    builder.add_doc_node(0, features=torch.randn(512))  # Research
    ↪  paper

    # Add edges
    builder.add_edge('query', 'expand', 'term', 0, "artificial")
    builder.add_edge('query', 'expand', 'term', 0, "intelligence")
    builder.add_edge('doc', 'contains', 'term', 0, "artificial")
    builder.add_edge('doc', 'contains', 'term', 0, "intelligence")
    builder.add_edge('term', 'related', 'term', "artificial",
    ↪  "intelligence")

    # Convert to PyG data
    data = builder.to_pyg_data()

    # Initialize model and optimizer
    model = NBHGEModel()
    optimizer = torch.optim.Adam(model.parameters(), lr=0.001)

    # Multi-phase training
```

68

```
for phase in [1, 2, 3]:
    for epoch in range(5):
        loss = train_phase(model, data, optimizer, phase=phase)
        print(f"Phase {phase} | Epoch {epoch+1} | Loss:
        ↪ {loss:.4f}")

# Generate expanded query embeddings
with torch.no_grad():
    expanded = model(data, target_query_ids=[0])

print(f"Expanded query vector shape: {expanded.shape}")

if __name__ == "__main__":
    main()
```

Key Implementation Details:

- **Heterogeneous Graph Construction:** The `GraphBuilder` class manages typed nodes and edges with automatic index mapping. Each node type (query/doc/term) receives specialized feature handling through separate embedding layers in the `NBHGEModel`.

- **Boundary Neuron Gates:** The `boundary_mlp` module computes gating weights between query-term pairs using concatenated features. These gates control how much expansion term information flows into the updated query representation.

- **Multi-Phase Training:** The `train_phase` function implements curriculum learning by progressively emphasizing different edge types. Phase 1 focuses on query-term expansions, Phase 2 incorporates click-through data, and Phase 3 trains on full graph connectivity.

- **Composite Loss Function:** The `NBHGELoss` combines expansion consistency (via cosine similarity) with document retrieval accuracy (via cross-entropy) to jointly optimize both query quality and end-task performance.

- **Heterogeneous Convolutions:** The model uses PyG's `HeteroConv` with GAT layers for query-related edges and GraphSAGE for term/document connections, allowing specialized message passing per relation type.

- **Dynamic Feature Updating:** During forward passes, query representations evolve by aggregating gated term features from their expansion neighborhoods, enabling context-aware query enrichment.

Chapter 10

Semi-Supervised Learning with Region-Agnostic Label Propagation

This chapter implements a Neuron-Boundary Heterogeneous Graph Engine (NBHGE) for semi-supervised learning through adaptive region interconnection. The system creates specialized data regions with boundary neurons that mediate cross-region information flow, enabling effective label propagation across heterogeneous subgraphs.

Key implementation steps:

- Partition input data into semantically coherent regions using feature clustering

- Initialize boundary neurons connecting adjacent regions through k-nearest neighbor matching

- Establish label confidence scores with anchor nodes from limited labeled examples

- Construct heterogeneous adjacency matrix with three connection types:

    - **Intra-region:** Dense connections within regions

- **Boundary:** Directed connections through boundary neurons
- **Inter-region:** Sparse connections between dissimilar regions

- Perform iterative label propagation with region-specific weighting

- Update confidence scores through boundary-mediated cross-region aggregation

Python Code Snippet

```python
import torch
import numpy as np
from sklearn.cluster import KMeans
from sklearn.metrics.pairwise import cosine_similarity
from scipy.sparse import lil_matrix, block_diag

# ------------------------------------------------------------
# Neuron-Boundary Heterogeneous Graph Engine (NBHGE)
# ------------------------------------------------------------
class RegionAgnosticPropagator:
    """
    Core NBHGE implementation with boundary neuron management
    and adaptive label propagation
    """
    def __init__(self, features, n_regions=3, boundary_size=5,
                 alpha=0.2, max_iters=50):
        """
        Args:
            features: Input node feature matrix [n_nodes,
            ↪    n_features]
            n_regions: Number of data partitions to create
            boundary_size: Number of boundary neurons per region
            ↪    pair
            alpha: Propagation damping factor (0-1)
            max_iters: Maximum propagation iterations
        """
        self.features = torch.FloatTensor(features)
        self.n_nodes = len(features)
        self.n_regions = n_regions
        self.boundary_size = boundary_size
        self.alpha = alpha
        self.max_iters = max_iters

        # Initialize regions and boundary neurons
        self.regions = self._create_regions()
        self.boundary_edges = self._add_boundary_neurons()
```

```python
        # Build heterogeneous adjacency matrix
        self.adj_matrix = self._build_adjacency_matrix()

    def _create_regions(self):
        """Partition data into specialized regions using feature
        ↪ clustering"""
        features_np = self.features.numpy()
        norms = np.linalg.norm(features_np, axis=1, keepdims=True)
        norms[norms == 0] = 1e-10
        features_normalized = features_np / norms
        kmeans = KMeans(n_clusters=self.n_regions)
        region_labels = kmeans.fit_predict(features_normalized)
        return [np.where(region_labels == i)[0] for i in
        ↪ range(self.n_regions)]

    def _add_boundary_neurons(self):
        """Create boundary neurons between adjacent regions"""
        boundaries = []
        for i in range(self.n_regions):
            for j in range(i+1, self.n_regions):
                # Find nearest neighbors between regions
                region_i = self.features[self.regions[i]].numpy()
                region_j = self.features[self.regions[j]].numpy()
                sim_matrix = cosine_similarity(region_i, region_j)

                # Select top boundary connections
                top_i = sim_matrix.argsort(axis=1)[:,
                ↪ -self.boundary_size:]
                top_j =
                ↪ sim_matrix.argsort(axis=0)[-self.boundary_size:,
                ↪ :]

                # Create bidirectional boundary edges
                for idx in range(len(self.regions[i])):
                    for jdx in top_i[idx]:
                        boundaries.append((self.regions[i][idx],
                        ↪ self.regions[j][jdx]))
                for jdx in range(len(self.regions[j])):
                    for idx in top_j[:, jdx]:
                        boundaries.append((self.regions[j][jdx],
                        ↪ self.regions[i][idx]))
        return list(set(boundaries))

    def _build_adjacency_matrix(self):
        """Construct heterogeneous adjacency matrix with region
        ↪ weighting"""
        adj = lil_matrix((self.n_nodes, self.n_nodes),
        ↪ dtype=np.float32)

        # Intra-region connections (dense)
        for region in self.regions:
            features_region = self.features[region].numpy()
```

```
        intra_sim = cosine_similarity(features_region)
        intra_sim = np.maximum(intra_sim, 0)
        np.fill_diagonal(intra_sim, 0)
        adj[np.ix_(region, region)] = intra_sim * 1.5

    # Boundary connections (directed)
    for src, tgt in self.boundary_edges:
        src_feat = self.features[src].numpy().reshape(1, -1)
        tgt_feat = self.features[tgt].numpy().reshape(1, -1)
        sim = cosine_similarity(src_feat, tgt_feat)[0][0]
        sim = max(sim, 0)
        adj[src, tgt] = sim * 2.0

    # Normalize and convert to dense matrix
    adj = adj.tocsr()
    row_sums = adj.sum(axis=1).A.reshape(-1)
    row_sums[row_sums == 0] = 1e-10
    adj = adj / row_sums[:, np.newaxis]
    return torch.FloatTensor(adj.toarray())

def propagate_labels(self, labeled_indices, labels, n_classes):
    """
    Perform boundary-mediated label propagation
    Args:
        labeled_indices: Indices of initially labeled nodes
        ↪   (torch.Tensor)
        labels: Corresponding class labels (0-based indices,
        ↪   torch.Tensor)
        n_classes: Total number of target classes
    Returns:
        Final confidence scores matrix [n_nodes, n_classes]
    """
    # Initialize confidence scores
    confidences = torch.zeros((self.n_nodes, n_classes))
    confidences[labeled_indices, labels] = 1.0

    # Propagation loop with boundary integration
    for _ in range(self.max_iters):
        new_conf = torch.zeros_like(confidences)

        # Intra-region propagation
        for region in self.regions:
            region_tensor = torch.from_numpy(region).long()
            region_conf = confidences[region_tensor]
            region_adj = self.adj_matrix[region_tensor][:,
            ↪   region_tensor]
            new_conf[region_tensor] += torch.mm(region_adj,
            ↪   region_conf)

        # Boundary-mediated cross-region propagation
        for src, tgt in self.boundary_edges:
            boundary_weight = self.adj_matrix[src, tgt]
            new_conf[tgt] += boundary_weight * confidences[src]
```

```python
            # Update with damping factor
            confidences = self.alpha * new_conf + (1 - self.alpha) *
            ↪  confidences

            # Maintain anchor labels
            confidences[labeled_indices, labels] = 1.0

        return confidences

# ----------------------------------------------------------------
# Dataset and Training Infrastructure
# ----------------------------------------------------------------
class SemiSupervisedDataset:
    """Manages partially labeled data for NBHGE"""
    def __init__(self, features, labels, label_mask):
        self.features = features
        self.labels = labels
        self.label_mask = label_mask

    def get_labeled_data(self):
        labeled_indices = torch.where(self.label_mask)[0]
        return labeled_indices, self.labels[labeled_indices]

def create_synthetic_data(n_samples=1000, n_features=128,
↪  n_classes=5):
    """Generate multimodal test data"""
    features = torch.randn(n_samples, n_features)
    labels = torch.randint(0, n_classes, (n_samples,))
    label_mask = torch.zeros(n_samples, dtype=bool)
    label_mask[:n_classes*5] = True
    return SemiSupervisedDataset(features, labels, label_mask)

# ----------------------------------------------------------------
# Execution Workflow
# ----------------------------------------------------------------
def main():
    # Configuration
    n_regions = 3
    boundary_size = 7
    n_classes = 5

    # Create synthetic dataset
    dataset = create_synthetic_data()
    labeled_idx, labels = dataset.get_labeled_data()

    # Initialize NBHGE
    propagator = RegionAgnosticPropagator(
        features=dataset.features,
        n_regions=n_regions,
        boundary_size=boundary_size
    )
```

```
# Perform label propagation
confidences = propagator.propagate_labels(
    labeled_indices=labeled_idx,
    labels=labels,
    n_classes=n_classes
)

# Evaluate results
preds = confidences.argmax(dim=1)
accuracy = (preds == dataset.labels).float().mean()
print(f"Final Accuracy: {accuracy.item()*100:.2f}%")
print("Class Distribution:\n", torch.histc(preds.float(),
↪    bins=n_classes))

if __name__ == "__main__":
    main()
```

Key Implementation Details:

- **Region Partitioning:** The `_create_regions` method uses K-means clustering on input features to create specialized data partitions, forming the basis for heterogeneous graph construction.

- **Boundary Neuron Creation:** The `_add_boundary_neurons` method identifies high-similarity node pairs between regions using cosine similarity, creating directed boundary connections that enable cross-region communication.

- **Heterogeneous Adjacency:** The `_build_adjacency_matrix` constructs a weighted graph with three connection types: boosted intra-region edges (1.5x), amplified boundary connections (2.0x), and sparse inter-region links.

- **Adaptive Propagation:** The `propagate_labels` method performs iterative confidence updates using a damping factor (`alpha`), separately processing intra-region and boundary-mediated updates while preserving anchor labels.

- **Multi-scale Weighting:** Boundary connections receive amplified weights in the adjacency matrix to prioritize cross-region information flow while maintaining strong intra-region signal propagation.

- **Anchoring Mechanism:** Labeled nodes maintain fixed confidence scores (1.0) throughout propagation through direct

76

matrix manipulation, ensuring supervision signal preservation.

- **Normalization Scheme:** Row-wise adjacency matrix normalization ensures stable numerical properties during propagation iterations while maintaining relative weight significance.

Chapter 11

Multi-Modal Data Fusion with NBHGE

This chapter presents a Neural-Boundary Heterogeneous Graph Engine (NBHGE) for multi-modal data integration. Our architecture establishes specialized sub-regions for different data types connected through adaptive boundary neurons that learn cross-modal relationships. The system dynamically routes information through modality-specific processors while maintaining coherent inter-domain connections.

Implementation pipeline:

- Construct heterogeneous graph with three core components:

    - **Region Encoders:** Domain-specific processors (CNN for images, LSTM for text, MLP for tabular)

    - **Boundary Neurons:** Trainable interfaces converting between modality embedding spaces

    - **Fusion Core:** Graph-based attention mechanism coordinating cross-region communication

- Implement modality alignment through:

    - Contrastive learning between boundary neuron outputs

    - Multi-task objectives with modality-specific reconstruction

    - Adaptive graph attention weights based on cross-modal correlation

- Enable complex queries across modalities using unified graph representation

Python Code Snippet

```python
import torch
import torch.nn as nn
import torch.nn.functional as F
from torch.utils.data import Dataset, DataLoader
from torchvision import transforms
from torch.nn.utils.rnn import pad_sequence
import numpy as np
from PIL import Image

# --------------------------------------------------------------
# NBHGE Core Architecture
# --------------------------------------------------------------
class NBHGEModel(nn.Module):
    """
    Neuron-Boundary Heterogeneous Graph Engine
    Regions: Image (CNN), Text (LSTM), Tabular (MLP)
    Boundary Neurons: img2txt, txt2tabular, tabular2img
    """
    def __init__(self, img_size, vocab_size, tabular_dim,
    ↪ embed_dim=256):
        super().__init__()

        # Region-specific encoders
        self.image_encoder = nn.Sequential(
            nn.Conv2d(3, 16, kernel_size=3, padding=1),
            nn.ReLU(),
            nn.MaxPool2d(2),
            nn.Conv2d(16, 32, kernel_size=3, padding=1),
            nn.ReLU(),
            nn.AdaptiveAvgPool2d((4,4)),
            nn.Flatten(),
            nn.Linear(32*4*4, embed_dim)
        )

        self.text_encoder = nn.LSTM(
            input_size=300,
            hidden_size=embed_dim//2,
            num_layers=2,
            bidirectional=True,
            batch_first=True
        )

        self.tabular_encoder = nn.Sequential(
            nn.Linear(tabular_dim, 512),
            nn.BatchNorm1d(512),
```

```python
    nn.ReLU(),
    nn.Dropout(0.2),
    nn.Linear(512, embed_dim)
)

# Boundary neurons (cross-modal adapters)
self.img2txt_boundary = nn.Sequential(
    nn.Linear(embed_dim, embed_dim*2),
    nn.GELU(),
    nn.Linear(embed_dim*2, embed_dim),
    nn.LayerNorm(embed_dim)
)

self.txt2tabular_boundary = nn.Sequential(
    nn.Linear(embed_dim, embed_dim*2),
    nn.GELU(),
    nn.Linear(embed_dim*2, embed_dim),
    nn.LayerNorm(embed_dim)
)

self.tabular2img_boundary = nn.Sequential(
    nn.Linear(embed_dim, embed_dim*2),
    nn.GELU(),
    nn.Linear(embed_dim*2, embed_dim),
    nn.LayerNorm(embed_dim)
)

# Cross-modal attention fusion
self.fusion_attn = nn.MultiheadAttention(
    embed_dim=embed_dim,
    num_heads=4,
    batch_first=True
)

# Reconstruction decoders
self.img_decoder = nn.Sequential(
    nn.Linear(embed_dim, 32*4*4),
    nn.Unflatten(1, (32,4,4)),
    nn.ConvTranspose2d(32, 16, kernel_size=3, stride=2,
    ↪  padding=1),
    nn.ReLU(),
    nn.ConvTranspose2d(16, 3, kernel_size=3, stride=2,
    ↪  padding=1)
)

self.txt_decoder_lstm = nn.LSTM(
    input_size=embed_dim,
    hidden_size=150,
    num_layers=2,
    bidirectional=True,
    batch_first=True
)
self.txt_decoder_linear = nn.Linear(300, 300)
```

```python
        self.tabular_decoder = nn.Sequential(
            nn.Linear(embed_dim, 512),
            nn.BatchNorm1d(512),
            nn.ReLU(),
            nn.Dropout(0.2),
            nn.Linear(512, tabular_dim)
        )

    def forward(self, img, txt, tabular):
        # Encode individual modalities
        img_emb = self.image_encoder(img)
        txt_emb, _ = self.text_encoder(txt)
        txt_emb = torch.mean(txt_emb, dim=1)
        tabular_emb = self.tabular_encoder(tabular)

        # Boundary neuron processing
        img2txt = self.img2txt_boundary(img_emb)
        txt2tabular = self.txt2tabular_boundary(txt_emb)
        tabular2img = self.tabular2img_boundary(tabular_emb)

        # Prepare fusion tokens
        fusion_tokens = torch.stack(
            [img_emb, txt_emb, tabular_emb,
             img2txt, txt2tabular, tabular2img],
            dim=1
        )

        # Cross-modal attention
        fused_emb, _ = self.fusion_attn(
            fusion_tokens, fusion_tokens, fusion_tokens
        )
        fused_emb = torch.mean(fused_emb, dim=1)

        # Reconstruct original modalities
        img_recon = self.img_decoder(fused_emb)
        txt_recon, _ =
        ↪ self.txt_decoder_lstm(fused_emb.unsqueeze(1).expand(-1,50,-1))
        txt_recon = self.txt_decoder_linear(txt_recon)
        tabular_recon = self.tabular_decoder(fused_emb)

        return {
            'img_emb': img_emb,
            'txt_emb': txt_emb,
            'tabular_emb': tabular_emb,
            'boundary_embs': [img2txt, txt2tabular, tabular2img],
            'reconstructions': (img_recon, txt_recon, tabular_recon)
        }

# ----------------------------------------------------------------
# Multimodal Dataset
# ----------------------------------------------------------------
class MultiModalDataset(Dataset):
```

```python
    def __init__(self, img_paths, texts, tabular_data, word_vecs):
        self.img_paths = img_paths
        self.texts = texts
        self.tabular_data = tabular_data
        self.word_vecs = word_vecs
        self.img_transform = transforms.Compose([
            transforms.Resize(64),
            transforms.ToTensor()
        ])

    def __len__(self):
        return len(self.img_paths)

    def __getitem__(self, idx):
        img = Image.open(self.img_paths[idx]).convert('RGB')
        img = self.img_transform(img)

        text = torch.stack([self.word_vecs[word] for word in
        ↪   self.texts[idx]])
        tabular = torch.FloatTensor(self.tabular_data[idx])

        return img, text, tabular

def collate_fn(batch):
    imgs, texts, tabulars = zip(*batch)
    imgs = torch.stack(imgs)
    tabulars = torch.stack(tabulars)

    text_lens = [t.shape[0] for t in texts]
    texts_padded = pad_sequence(texts, batch_first=True)

    return imgs, texts_padded, tabulars, text_lens

# ------------------------------------------------------------
# Training Logic
# ------------------------------------------------------------
def nbhge_loss(outputs, inputs, text_lens):
    img_loss = F.mse_loss(outputs['reconstructions'][0], inputs[0])
    txt_loss = sum([
        F.cosine_similarity(outputs['reconstructions'][1][i,:l],
        ↪   inputs[1][i,:l]).mean()
        for i, l in enumerate(text_lens)
    ]) / len(text_lens)
    tabular_loss = F.mse_loss(outputs['reconstructions'][2],
    ↪   inputs[2])

    boundary_embs = outputs['boundary_embs']
    align_loss = sum([
        F.cosine_similarity(boundary_embs[0], boundary_embs[1],
        ↪   dim=1).mean() +
        F.cosine_similarity(boundary_embs[1], boundary_embs[2],
        ↪   dim=1).mean()
    ])
```

```python
    return {
        'total': img_loss - txt_loss + tabular_loss + align_loss,
        'img_recon': img_loss,
        'txt_recon': -txt_loss,
        'tabular_recon': tabular_loss,
        'boundary_align': align_loss
    }

def train_epoch(model, loader, optimizer, device):
    model.train()
    total_loss = 0
    for imgs, texts, tabulars, text_lens in loader:
        imgs = imgs.to(device)
        texts = texts.to(device)
        tabulars = tabulars.to(device)

        optimizer.zero_grad()
        outputs = model(imgs, texts, tabulars)
        loss_dict = nbhge_loss(outputs, (imgs, texts, tabulars),
        ↪   text_lens)

        loss_dict['total'].backward()
        optimizer.step()

        total_loss += loss_dict['total'].item()
    return total_loss / len(loader)

# -------------------------------------------------------------
# Main Execution
# -------------------------------------------------------------
def main():
    device = torch.device('cuda' if torch.cuda.is_available() else
    ↪   'cpu')

    word_vecs = {'cat': torch.randn(300), 'dog': torch.randn(300)}
    dataset = MultiModalDataset(
        img_paths=['img1.jpg', 'img2.jpg'],
        texts=[['cat', 'sitting'], ['dog', 'running']],
        tabular_data=[[0.5, 1.2], [0.7, 0.9]],
        word_vecs=word_vecs
    )

    loader = DataLoader(
        dataset, batch_size=2, collate_fn=collate_fn, shuffle=True
    )

    model = NBHGEModel(
        img_size=(3,64,64),
        vocab_size=len(word_vecs),
        tabular_dim=2
    ).to(device)
```

```
    optimizer = torch.optim.AdamW(model.parameters(), lr=1e-4)

    for epoch in range(1, 6):
        avg_loss = train_epoch(model, loader, optimizer, device)
        print(f"Epoch {epoch} | Loss: {avg_loss:.4f}")
        print_model_stats(model)

def print_model_stats(model):
    for name, param in model.named_parameters():
        if 'boundary' in name:
            print(f"{name}: {param.data.norm().item():.4f}")

if __name__ == "__main__":
    main()
```

Key Implementation Details:

- **Modality-Specific Regions:** The `NBHGEModel` class implements dedicated processing paths through `image_encoder`, `text_encoder`, and `tabular_encoder` to handle domain-specific feature extraction.

- **Adaptive Boundary Neurons:** Three boundary modules (`img2txt_boundary`, `txt2tabular_boundary`, `tabular2img_boundary`) translate embeddings between modalities using learned nonlinear projections with layer normalization.

- **Cross-Modal Attention Fusion:** The `fusion_attn` module enables all region embeddings and boundary-transformed representations to interact through multi-head attention, creating context-aware unified representations.

- **Multi-Objective Training:** The custom `nbhge_loss` combines reconstruction losses for each modality with boundary alignment penalties that enforce semantic consistency across domains.

- **Dynamic Padding Handling:** The dataset's `collate_fn` manages variable-length text sequences while preserving image and tabular data integrity through proper tensor stacking.

- **Boundary Activation Monitoring:** The `print_model_stats` helper tracks boundary neuron weight norms to detect learning patterns in cross-modal translation pathways.

84

Chapter 12

Temporal Graph Forecasting with Boundary Neurons

This chapter presents a Temporal Graph Neural Network architecture that leverages boundary neurons to model time-evolving relationships in heterogeneous graphs. Our Neuron-Boundary Heterogeneous Graph Engine (NBHGE) dynamically partitions temporal graphs into localized regions while maintaining inter-region connectivity through specialized boundary neurons that capture state transitions across temporal partitions.

Key implementation strategy:

- Temporal graph segmentation into snapshots based on time windows

- Boundary neuron initialization at region interfaces

- Dual processing streams:

    - **Node State Updates:** Gated message passing within temporal regions
    - **Boundary Synchronization:** Cross-region state propagation through boundary neurons

- Rolling parameter updates for boundary neurons using recent observations

- Hybrid loss combining node state prediction and edge existence forecasting

- Temporal attention mechanism for importance weighting across historical states

Python Code Snippet

```python
import torch
import torch.nn as nn
import torch.nn.functional as F
from torch_geometric.nn import GATConv
from torch_geometric.data import Dataset, DataLoader
import numpy as np


# ------------------------------------------------------------
# Neuron-Boundary Heterogeneous Graph Engine (NBHGE)
# ------------------------------------------------------------
class NBHGEModel(nn.Module):
    """
    Temporal graph forecasting with boundary neuron synchronization
    Key components:
    - Region-specific GNN processors
    - Boundary neuron state buffers
    - Temporal attention fusion
    - Rolling boundary updates
    """
    def __init__(self, node_feat_dim, edge_feat_dim, boundary_size,
                 num_regions, hist_len, forecast_len, device):
        super().__init__()
        self.boundary_size = boundary_size
        self.num_regions = num_regions
        self.hist_len = hist_len
        self.device = device

        # Region processors with shared parameters
        self.node_encoder = nn.GRU(node_feat_dim, boundary_size,
        ↪   batch_first=True)
        self.edge_processor = GATConv(boundary_size,
        ↪   boundary_size//2, heads=2)

        # Boundary neuron infrastructure
        self.boundary_states = nn.ParameterDict({
            f'region_{i}': nn.Parameter(torch.randn(node_feat_dim,
            ↪   boundary_size))
            for i in range(num_regions)
        })
        self.boundary_mlp = nn.Sequential(
            nn.Linear(2*boundary_size, boundary_size),
            nn.LeakyReLU(),
```

86

```python
            nn.LayerNorm(boundary_size)
        )

        # Temporal attention and forecasting
        self.temporal_attn = nn.MultiheadAttention(boundary_size, 4,
        ↪  batch_first=True)
        self.forecast_decoder = nn.Linear(boundary_size * hist_len,
        ↪  boundary_size)

        # State synchronization parameters
        self.update_gate = nn.Linear(3*(boundary_size//2),
        ↪  boundary_size)
        self.reset_gate = nn.Linear(boundary_size, boundary_size)

    def forward(self, region_data, boundary_masks):
        """
        Process temporal graph regions with boundary mediation
        Args:
            region_data: List of (node_features, edge_index,
            ↪  edge_attr) per region
            boundary_masks: List of mask matrices indicating
            ↪  boundary nodes
        Returns:
            node_preds: Predicted node states for t+1
            edge_preds: Predicted edge existences
            boundary_states: Updated boundary neuron parameters
        """
        batch_size = region_data[0][0].size(0)
        all_boundaries = []
        region_outputs = []

        # Process each temporal region
        for region_idx, (nodes, edges, _) in enumerate(region_data):
            # Encode node features with temporal context
            node_emb, _ = self.node_encoder(nodes)

            # Process graph structure with attention
            current_nodes = node_emb[:, -1, :]
            edge_emb = self.edge_processor(current_nodes, edges)

            # Boundary neuron integration
            boundary_matrix =
            ↪  self.boundary_states[f'region_{region_idx}']
            masked_nodes = torch.matmul(boundary_masks[region_idx],
            ↪  boundary_matrix)
            fused_nodes = self.boundary_mlp(
                torch.cat([current_nodes, masked_nodes], dim=-1)
            )

            # Store boundary states for synchronization
            region_outputs.append(fused_nodes)
            boundary = fused_nodes[:, :self.boundary_size//2]
            all_boundaries.append(boundary)
```

```python
        # Synchronize boundaries across regions
        synced_boundaries =
        ↪   self._synchronize_boundaries(all_boundaries)

        # Temporal attention fusion
        hist_states = torch.stack(region_outputs, dim=1)
        attn_out, _ = self.temporal_attn(hist_states, hist_states,
        ↪   hist_states)

        # Generate forecasts
        forecast = self.forecast_decoder(attn_out.view(batch_size,
        ↪   -1))
        node_preds = forecast[..., :node_emb.size(-1)]
        edge_preds = forecast[..., node_emb.size(-1):]

        # Update boundary states (rolling window)
        self._update_boundary_parameters(synced_boundaries)

        return node_preds, edge_preds.squeeze(), synced_boundaries

    def _synchronize_boundaries(self, boundaries):
        """Coordinate boundary states between adjacent regions"""
        synced = []
        for i in range(len(boundaries)):
            prev = boundaries[i-1] if i > 0 else
            ↪   torch.zeros_like(boundaries[0])
            next_ = boundaries[i+1] if i < len(boundaries)-1 else
            ↪   torch.zeros_like(boundaries[0])
            combined = torch.cat([prev, boundaries[i], next_],
            ↪   dim=-1)
            update = torch.sigmoid(self.update_gate(combined))
            reset = torch.sigmoid(self.reset_gate(torch.cat([prev,
            ↪   boundaries[i]], dim=-1)))
            new_state = update * boundaries[i] + (1 - update) *
            ↪   reset * prev
            synced.append(new_state)
        return torch.stack(synced, dim=1)

    def _update_boundary_parameters(self, new_states):
        """Rolling update of boundary neuron parameters"""
        with torch.no_grad():
            for i in range(self.num_regions):
                self.boundary_states[f'region_{i}'].data = (
                    0.8 * self.boundary_states[f'region_{i}'].data +
                    0.2 * new_states[:, i, :].mean(dim=0)
                )

# -----------------------------------------------------------
# Temporal Graph Dataset
# -----------------------------------------------------------
class TemporalGraphDataset(Dataset):
    """Loads time-sliced graph data with boundary annotations"""
```

```python
    def __init__(self, temporal_edges, node_features, num_regions,
    ↪ hist_len):
        self.temporal_edges = temporal_edges
        self.node_features = node_features
        self.num_regions = num_regions
        self.hist_len = hist_len
        self.boundary_masks = self._detect_boundaries()

    def _detect_boundaries(self):
        """Identify nodes connecting temporal regions"""
        masks = []
        for i in range(self.num_regions):
            region_edges = self.temporal_edges[i]
            unique_nodes = torch.unique(region_edges)
            mask = torch.zeros_like(self.node_features[0])
            mask[unique_nodes] = 1.0
            masks.append(mask)
        return masks

    def __len__(self):
        return len(self.temporal_edges) - self.hist_len

    def __getitem__(self, idx):
        region_slice = slice(idx, idx + self.hist_len)
        target_slice = slice(idx + self.hist_len, idx +
        ↪ self.hist_len + 1)

        hist_nodes = [self.node_features[i] for i in
        ↪ range(*region_slice.indices(len(self)))]
        hist_edges = [self.temporal_edges[i] for i in
        ↪ range(*region_slice.indices(len(self)))]
        target_data = (self.node_features[target_slice],
                       self.temporal_edges[target_slice])

        return (hist_nodes, hist_edges), target_data,
        ↪ self.boundary_masks


# ----------------------------------------------------------------
# Training and Forecasting
# ----------------------------------------------------------------
def train_epoch(model, loader, optimizer, device):
    model.train()
    total_loss = 0
    for (hist_nodes, hist_edges), (tgt_nodes, tgt_edges), masks in
    ↪ loader:
        hist_nodes = [n.to(device) for n in hist_nodes]
        hist_edges = [e.to(device) for e in hist_edges]
        masks = [m.to(device) for m in masks]

        optimizer.zero_grad()
        node_preds, edge_preds, _ = model(zip(hist_nodes,
        ↪ hist_edges, masks), masks)
```

```python
            node_loss = F.mse_loss(node_preds, tgt_nodes.to(device))
            edge_loss = F.binary_cross_entropy_with_logits(
                edge_preds, tgt_edges.float().to(device)
            )
            total_loss = 0.7*node_loss + 0.3*edge_loss

            total_loss.backward()
            optimizer.step()

    return total_loss.item()

def forecast(model, init_states, steps, device):
    """Rolling forecast with boundary state propagation"""
    model.eval()
    predictions = []
    current_states = init_states

    with torch.no_grad():
        for _ in range(steps):
            next_nodes, next_edges, current_states =
            ↪   model(current_states)
            predictions.append((next_nodes.cpu(), next_edges.cpu()))
            current_states = (next_nodes.unsqueeze(0),
                              current_states[1][1:],
                              current_states[2][1:])

    return predictions


# ---------------------------------------------------------------
# Main Execution
# ---------------------------------------------------------------
def main():
    DEVICE = torch.device('cuda' if torch.cuda.is_available() else
    ↪   'cpu')
    NUM_NODES = 1000
    BOUNDARY_SIZE = 64
    HIST_LEN = 6
    FORECAST_LEN = 3

    node_feats = torch.randn(100, NUM_NODES, 32)
    edge_list = [torch.randint(0, NUM_NODES, (2, 50)) for _ in
    ↪   range(100)]

    dataset = TemporalGraphDataset(edge_list, node_feats,
    ↪   num_regions=5, hist_len=HIST_LEN)
    model = NBHGEModel(
        node_feat_dim=32,
        edge_feat_dim=16,
        boundary_size=BOUNDARY_SIZE,
        num_regions=5,
        hist_len=HIST_LEN,
        forecast_len=FORECAST_LEN,
        device=DEVICE
```

```
).to(DEVICE)

optimizer = torch.optim.AdamW(model.parameters(), lr=1e-3)
loader = DataLoader(dataset, batch_size=32, shuffle=True)

for epoch in range(1, 11):
    loss = train_epoch(model, loader, optimizer, DEVICE)
    print(f"Epoch {epoch} | Total Loss: {loss:.4f}")

    test_sample = dataset[0][0]
    predictions = forecast(model, test_sample,
    ↪ steps=FORECAST_LEN, device=DEVICE)
    print(f"Forecast shape: {predictions[0][0].shape}")

if __name__ == "__main__":
    main()
```

Key Implementation Details:

- **Boundary Neuron Architecture:** The `NBHGEModel` maintains region-specific boundary parameters through `boundary_states` matrices that are dynamically updated via `_update_boundary_parameters`. These matrices mediate inter-region communication through learned linear transformations.

- **Dual Processing Streams:** The model separates node feature encoding (via GRU) from edge processing (via GAT-Conv), followed by boundary-aware fusion using `boundary_mlp` to combine internal and boundary states.

- **Temporal Synchronization:** The `_synchronize_boundaries` method implements gated state passing between adjacent temporal regions using update and reset gates similar to GRU mechanisms, but applied across spatial boundaries.

- **Rolling State Updates:** Boundary neuron parameters receive continuous updates through `_update_boundary_parameters` using an 80-20 moving average between historical and new observed states.

- **Hybrid Forecasting:** The model jointly predicts node states (via MSE loss) and edge existence (via BCE loss) through separate decoder heads fed by temporal attention outputs.

- **Memory Efficiency:** The `TemporalGraphDataset` implements boundary detection through `_detect_boundaries` by tracking nodes appearing in multiple temporal regions, avoiding explicit storage of boundary annotations.

- **Autoregressive Forecasting:** The `forecast` function enables multi-step prediction by recursively feeding model outputs back into the input states while maintaining boundary neuron coherence.

Chapter 13

Network Flow Optimization with Subgraph Collaboration

This chapter implements a flow optimization framework using the Neuron-Boundary Heterogeneous Graph Engine (NBHGE). Our architecture models complex networks as interconnected subgraphs with specialized boundary neurons that negotiate flow constraints between regions. The system learns optimal routing strategies through coordinated updates of local flow potentials and boundary negotiation parameters.

Key implementation steps:

- Partition network into functional subgraphs (e.g., highway segments, warehouse clusters)

- Initialize boundary neurons at subgraph interfaces with trainable negotiation weights

- Encode local capacity constraints and flow potential embeddings for each subgraph

- Implement message passing between boundary neurons and local flow predictors

- Optimize using multi-component loss:

- Flow demand satisfaction within subgraphs
- Capacity constraint adherence
- Boundary flow consistency penalties
- Global congestion minimization

- Update boundary neuron weights through gradient-based alignment of inter-region flows

Python Code Snippet

```python
import torch
import torch.nn as nn
import torch.optim as optim
from torch_geometric.data import Data
from torch_geometric.nn import MessagePassing
from torch_geometric.utils import add_self_loops, degree
import numpy as np

# ------------------------------------------------------------
# Neuron-Boundary Heterogeneous Graph Engine (NBHGE)
# ------------------------------------------------------------
class NBHGEFlowOptimizer(nn.Module):
    """
    Core NBHGE architecture for flow optimization with:
    - Region-specific GNNs for local flow prediction
    - Boundary negotiation neurons between subgraphs
    - Capacity-aware message passing with penalty terms
    """
    def __init__(self, num_regions, node_features, boundary_dim,
                 capacity_constraints, device):
        super().__init__()
        self.device = device
        self.num_regions = num_regions
        self.capacity_constraints = capacity_constraints.to(device)

        # Region-specific flow predictors
        self.region_gnns = nn.ModuleList([
            RegionGNN(node_features, 64, 32)
            for _ in range(num_regions)
        ])

        # Boundary negotiation parameters
        self.boundary_neurons = nn.Parameter(
            torch.randn(num_regions, num_regions, boundary_dim)
        )
        self.boundary_attention = nn.MultiheadAttention(
            boundary_dim, 4, batch_first=True
        )
```

```python
        # Flow potential embeddings
        self.flow_embeddings = nn.Embedding(num_regions, 32)
        self.capacity_proj = nn.Linear(1, 32)

        # Output layers
        self.flow_predictor = nn.Sequential(
            nn.Linear(128, 64),
            nn.ReLU(),
            nn.Linear(64, 1)
        )

    def forward(self, region_data, adj_matrix):
        """
        Process flow optimization through subgraph collaboration
        region_data: List of Data objects for each subgraph
        adj_matrix: Region connectivity matrix
        """
        batch_size = region_data[0].x.size(0)

        # 1. Process local flows within each region
        local_flows = []
        capacity_features = []
        for i, gnn in enumerate(self.region_gnns):
            flow = gnn(region_data[i].x, region_data[i].edge_index)
            local_flows.append(flow)
            # Capacity features with safety margin
            capacity = torch.sigmoid(self.capacity_proj(
                self.capacity_constraints[i] * 0.9 - flow.abs()
            ))
            capacity_features.append(capacity)

        # 2. Boundary neuron communication
        boundary_signals = []
        for i in range(self.num_regions):
            for j in range(self.num_regions):
                if adj_matrix[i,j] > 0 and i != j:
                    # Negotiate boundary flows using attention
                    signal = self._negotiate_boundary(
                        local_flows[i], local_flows[j],
                        self.boundary_neurons[i,j],
                        capacity_features[i], capacity_features[j]
                    )
                    boundary_signals.append(signal)

        # 3. Aggregate global flow state
        global_state = torch.cat([
            torch.mean(torch.stack(local_flows), dim=0),
            torch.mean(torch.stack(capacity_features), dim=0),
            torch.mean(torch.stack(boundary_signals), dim=0)
        ], dim=-1)

        # 4. Final flow prediction with capacity constraints
```

```python
        predicted_flow = self.flow_predictor(global_state)
        return predicted_flow.squeeze()

    def _negotiate_boundary(self, flow_i, flow_j, boundary_weight,
                            capacity_i, capacity_j):
        """
        Boundary negotiation between two regions using:
        - Current flow estimates from both sides
        - Shared boundary neuron weights
        - Capacity utilization features
        """
        # Compute flow differential
        flow_diff = (flow_i - flow_j).unsqueeze(1)

        # Capacity-aware attention
        key = torch.cat([capacity_i, capacity_j], dim=-1)
        value = torch.cat([flow_i, flow_j], dim=-1)
        attn_output, _ = self.boundary_attention(
            boundary_weight.expand(flow_diff.size(0), -1, -1),
            key.unsqueeze(1),
            value.unsqueeze(1)
        )

        # Adjust flow differential with attention weights
        adjusted_diff = flow_diff * attn_output.squeeze()
        return torch.mean(adjusted_diff, dim=-1)

    def compute_loss(self, predicted, actual, region_data):
        """
        Multi-component loss function for NBHGE:
        - Flow prediction accuracy
        - Capacity constraint adherence
        - Boundary alignment penalties
        """
        # Base flow prediction loss
        flow_loss = nn.MSELoss()(predicted, actual)

        # Capacity constraint violation penalty
        capacity_penalty = 0
        for i, data in enumerate(region_data):
            utilization = torch.mean(
                predicted[data.node_mask] /
                ↪ self.capacity_constraints[i]
            )
            capacity_penalty += torch.relu(utilization - 0.85)  #
            ↪ 15% safety margin

        # Boundary consistency loss
        boundary_loss = torch.mean(
            torch.stack([self._boundary_alignment(region_data[i],
            ↪ region_data[j])
                        for i in range(self.num_regions)
                        for j in range(self.num_regions) if i != j])
```

```
        )
        return flow_loss + 0.3*capacity_penalty + 0.2*boundary_loss

    def _boundary_alignment(self, region_i, region_j):
        """
        Measures flow consistency at shared boundaries between
        ↪ regions
        """
        boundary_nodes_i = region_i.boundary_nodes
        boundary_nodes_j = region_j.boundary_nodes
        flow_diff = torch.mean(
            region_i.x[boundary_nodes_i] -
            ↪ region_j.x[boundary_nodes_j]
        )
        return torch.abs(flow_diff)


# --------------------------------------------------------------
# Region-Specific GNN Component
# --------------------------------------------------------------
class RegionGNN(MessagePassing):
    """
    Custom message passing layer for learning local flow potentials
    Implements capacity-aware aggregation with edge normalization
    """
    def __init__(self, in_channels, hidden_dim, out_dim):
        super().__init__(aggr='mean')
        self.lin = nn.Linear(in_channels, hidden_dim)
        self.flow_encoder = nn.Sequential(
            nn.Linear(hidden_dim*2, out_dim),
            nn.ReLU()
        )
        self.capacity_encoder = nn.Linear(1, hidden_dim)

    def forward(self, x, edge_index):
        # Add self-loops for stability
        edge_index, _ = add_self_loops(edge_index,
        ↪ num_nodes=x.size(0))

        # Transform node features
        x = self.lin(x)

        # Start message passing
        return self.propagate(edge_index, x=x)

    def message(self, x_i, x_j, edge_index):
        # Compute normalized message weights
        row, col = edge_index
        deg = degree(col, x_i.size(0), dtype=x_i.dtype)
        deg_inv_sqrt = deg.pow(-0.5)
        norm = deg_inv_sqrt[row] * deg_inv_sqrt[col]

        # Capacity-adjusted message
```

97

```
            return norm.view(-1, 1) * (x_i + x_j) / 2

    def update(self, aggr_out):
        return self.flow_encoder(aggr_out)


# --------------------------------------------------------------
# Dataset and Training Infrastructure
# --------------------------------------------------------------
class FlowDataset(Dataset):
    """
    Represents network flow data with multiple subgraph regions
    Stores node features, edge indices, and boundary node masks
    """
    def __init__(self, network_configs, flow_data, capacity_limits):
        self.regions = network_configs
        self.flow_data = flow_data
        self.capacity_limits = capacity_limits

    def __len__(self):
        return len(self.flow_data)

    def __getitem__(self, idx):
        region_data = []
        for config in self.regions:
            x = torch.tensor(config['node_features'],
            ↪    dtype=torch.float)
            edge_index = torch.tensor(config['edges'],
            ↪    dtype=torch.long).t().contiguous()
            boundary_nodes = torch.tensor(config['boundary_nodes'],
            ↪    dtype=torch.long)
            region_data.append(Data(
                x=x, edge_index=edge_index,
                boundary_nodes=boundary_nodes,
                node_mask=torch.tensor(config['node_mask'],
                ↪    dtype=torch.bool)
            ))
        return region_data, torch.tensor(self.flow_data[idx],
        ↪    dtype=torch.float)


def train_nbhge(model, dataloader, epochs=100, lr=0.001):
    optimizer = optim.AdamW(model.parameters(), lr=lr)
    scheduler = optim.lr_scheduler.ReduceLROnPlateau(optimizer,
    ↪    'min', patience=5)

    for epoch in range(epochs):
        model.train()
        total_loss = 0
        for batch in dataloader:
            region_data, true_flows = batch
            optimizer.zero_grad()

            # Forward pass through all regions
```

```python
            pred_flows = model(region_data,
            ↪    adj_matrix=get_adjacency())

            # Compute multi-component loss
            loss = model.compute_loss(pred_flows, true_flows,
            ↪    region_data)

            loss.backward()
            nn.utils.clip_grad_norm_(model.parameters(), 1.0)
            optimizer.step()
            total_loss += loss.item()

        scheduler.step(total_loss)
        print(f"Epoch {epoch+1} | Loss:
        ↪    {total_loss/len(dataloader):.4f}")

def evaluate_flows(model, dataloader):
    model.eval()
    congestion_scores = []
    with torch.no_grad():
        for batch in dataloader:
            region_data, true_flows = batch
            pred_flows = model(region_data,
            ↪    adj_matrix=get_adjacency())

            # Calculate capacity utilization rates
            for i, data in enumerate(region_data):
                utilization = pred_flows[data.node_mask] /
                ↪    model.capacity_constraints[i]
                congestion = torch.mean(torch.relu(utilization -
                ↪    1.0))
                congestion_scores.append(congestion.item())

    print(f"Network Congestion Score:
    ↪    {np.mean(congestion_scores):.2%}")

# ------------------------------------------------------------
# Main Execution
# ------------------------------------------------------------
def main():
    # Example network configuration
    highway_config = {
        'node_features': [...],
        'edges': [...],
        'boundary_nodes': [5, 6, 7],
        'node_mask': [...]
    }

    city_roads_config = {
        'node_features': [...],
        'edges': [...],
        'boundary_nodes': [0, 1],
        'node_mask': [...]
```

```
}

# Initialize NBHGE model
device = torch.device('cuda' if torch.cuda.is_available() else
↪  'cpu')
model = NBHGEFlowOptimizer(
    num_regions=2,
    node_features=8,
    boundary_dim=64,
    capacity_constraints=torch.tensor([1500, 800]),  # Example
    ↪  capacities
    device=device
).to(device)

# Prepare dataset and dataloader
dataset = FlowDataset([highway_config, city_roads_config], ...)
dataloader = DataLoader(dataset, batch_size=32, shuffle=True)

# Train and evaluate
train_nbhge(model, dataloader, epochs=50)
evaluate_flows(model, dataloader)

if __name__ == "__main__":
    main()
```

Key Implementation Details:

- **Heterogeneous Graph Structure:** The NBHGEFlowOptimizer
  manages multiple RegionGNN instances while coordinating
  boundary negotiations through learned boundary_neurons
  parameters.

- **Boundary Negotiation Mechanism:** The _negotiate_boundary
  method implements capacity-aware attention between regions
  using multi-head attention over boundary neuron weights and
  current flow states.

- **Flow Potential Learning:** Region-specific GNNs process
  local network topologies using custom message passing that
  incorporates degree normalization and capacity projections.

- **Multi-Objective Loss:** The compute_loss function combines flow prediction accuracy, capacity constraint penalties,
  and boundary alignment costs to balance local/global optimization.

- **Capacity-Aware Messaging:** The `RegionGNN` incorporates capacity limitations into its message passing through specialized projection layers and safety margin calculations.

- **Dynamic Gradient Updates:** Boundary neuron weights receive gradient signals from both flow prediction errors and inter-region consistency penalties, enabling collaborative optimization.

Chapter 14

Active Learning with Region-Specific Curiosity

This chapter implements an active learning system using Neuron-Boundary Heterogeneous Graph Engine (NBHGE) that strategically selects informative samples through boundary-aware uncertainty quantification. The architecture employs specialized boundary neurons that monitor information flow between data regions, enabling targeted queries that maximize learning efficiency.

Key implementation steps:

- Partition input data into semantic regions using feature clustering

- Implement boundary-aware graph neural network with:

  - **Intra-Region Processing:** Standard message passing within clusters
  - **Inter-Region Processing:** Boundary neuron-mediated cross-cluster communication

- Track boundary confusion metrics through activation variance analysis

- Develop region-curious sampling policy prioritizing high-variance boundaries

- Dynamically update labeled set based on boundary neuron signals

Python Code Snippet

```python
import torch
import torch.nn as nn
import torch.nn.functional as F
import numpy as np
from collections import defaultdict
from sklearn.cluster import KMeans


# ------------------------------------------------------------
# Neuron-Boundary Heterogeneous Graph Engine (NBHGE)
# ------------------------------------------------------------
class NBHGE(nn.Module):
    """

    Implements boundary-mediated graph processing with:
    - Region-specific message passing
    - Boundary neuron interfaces between regions
    - Automatic confusion tracking at region boundaries
    """
    def __init__(self, input_dim, hidden_dim, num_regions,
    ↪ num_classes):
        super().__init__()
        # Message passing layers
        self.intra_layer = nn.Linear(input_dim, hidden_dim)  #
        ↪ Within-region processing
        self.boundary_layer = nn.Linear(input_dim, hidden_dim)  #
        ↪ Cross-region processing
        self.classifier = nn.Linear(hidden_dim, num_classes)  #
        ↪ Final prediction layer

        # Boundary monitoring system
        self.confusion_tracker = defaultdict(float)

    def forward(self, x, edge_index, regions):
        """

        Process graph with boundary-aware message passing:
        1. Separate intra-region and cross-region messages
        2. Track boundary neuron activation patterns
        3. Update node representations with region context
        """
        row, col = edge_index
        messages = torch.zeros(x.size(0),
        ↪ self.intra_layer.out_features,
                             device=x.device, dtype=x.dtype)
        boundary_activations = defaultdict(list)

        # Process all graph edges
```

```python
        for i in range(edge_index.size(1)):
            src, dst = row[i].item(), col[i].item()
            src_region = regions[src].item()
            dst_region = regions[dst].item()

            if src_region == dst_region:
                # Intra-region message passing
                msg = self.intra_layer(x[src])
            else:
                # Cross-region through boundary neuron
                msg = self.boundary_layer(x[src])
                boundary_activations[(src_region,
                ↪   dst_region)].append(msg)

            messages[dst] += msg  # Aggregate messages

        # Update boundary confusion metrics
        self._update_confusion_tracker(boundary_activations)

        # Final node representations and predictions
        x_updated = F.relu(messages)
        return self.classifier(x_updated)

    def _update_confusion_tracker(self, boundary_activations):
        """Calculate variance in boundary neuron activations as
        ↪   confusion metric"""
        self.confusion_tracker.clear()
        for (r1, r2), activations in boundary_activations.items():
            if activations:
                act_tensor = torch.stack(activations)
                self.confusion_tracker[(r1, r2)] =
                ↪   act_tensor.var(dim=0,
                ↪   unbiased=False).mean().item()


# ------------------------------------------------------------
# Active Learning Infrastructure
# ------------------------------------------------------------
class RegionCuriositySampler:
    """Selects nodes at high-confusion boundaries using NBHGE
    ↪   signals"""
    def __init__(self, model, regions, labeled_mask):
        self.model = model
        self.regions = regions
        self.labeled_mask = labeled_mask

    def query_nodes(self, num_query=5):
        """Select unlabeled nodes near most confused boundaries"""
        # Identify top confused region boundaries
        boundary_confusions = sorted(
            self.model.confusion_tracker.items(),
            key=lambda x: -x[1]
        )[:3]  # Select top 3 confused boundaries
```

```python
        # Collect candidate regions
        candidate_regions = set()
        for (r1, r2), _ in boundary_confusions:
            candidate_regions.add(r1)
            candidate_regions.add(r2)

        # Find unlabeled nodes in candidate regions
        candidate_nodes = [
            n for n in range(len(self.regions))
            if not self.labeled_mask[n] and self.regions[n].item()
            ↪ in candidate_regions
        ]

        # Handle insufficient candidates
        num_samples = min(num_query, len(candidate_nodes))
        if num_samples == 0:
            return np.array([], dtype=int)

        # Random sampling from candidates
        return np.random.choice(candidate_nodes, size=num_samples,
        ↪ replace=False)


# ----------------------------------------------------------------
# Graph Dataset Manager
# ----------------------------------------------------------------
class DynamicGraphDataset:
    """Manages evolving graph with active labeling"""
    def __init__(self, num_nodes, feature_dim, num_regions):
        # Generate synthetic graph data
        self.x = torch.randn(num_nodes, feature_dim)
        self.edge_index = self._generate_edges(num_nodes)
        self.regions = self._cluster_regions(num_regions)
        self.labels = torch.randint(0, 2, (num_nodes,))
        self.labeled_mask = torch.zeros(num_nodes, dtype=torch.bool)

    def _generate_edges(self, num_nodes):
        """Create random adjacency matrix (replace with real
        ↪ data)"""
        return torch.randint(0, num_nodes, (2, num_nodes*2))

    def _cluster_regions(self, num_regions):
        """Partition nodes into semantic regions"""
        kmeans = KMeans(n_clusters=num_regions)
        return torch.tensor(kmeans.fit_predict(self.x.numpy()),
        ↪ dtype=torch.long)

    def update_labels(self, new_indices):
        """Mark selected nodes as labeled"""
        self.labeled_mask[new_indices] = True


# ----------------------------------------------------------------
# Training and Active Learning Loop
# ----------------------------------------------------------------
```

```python
def main():
    # Configuration
    NUM_NODES = 1000
    FEATURE_DIM = 128
    NUM_REGIONS = 10
    HIDDEN_DIM = 256
    NUM_CLASSES = 2
    INIT_LABELS = 20
    QUERY_SIZE = 10
    EPOCHS_PER_CYCLE = 5

    # Initialize system components
    dataset = DynamicGraphDataset(NUM_NODES, FEATURE_DIM,
    ↪    NUM_REGIONS)
    model = NBHGE(FEATURE_DIM, HIDDEN_DIM, NUM_REGIONS, NUM_CLASSES)
    optimizer = torch.optim.Adam(model.parameters(), lr=0.001)

    # Initial labeling
    initial_labels = np.random.choice(NUM_NODES, INIT_LABELS,
    ↪    replace=False)
    dataset.update_labels(initial_labels)

    # Active learning cycles
    for cycle in range(10):
        # Train current model
        model.train()
        for _ in range(EPOCHS_PER_CYCLE):
            optimizer.zero_grad()
            logits = model(dataset.x, dataset.edge_index,
            ↪    dataset.regions)
            loss = F.cross_entropy(logits[dataset.labeled_mask],
            ↪    dataset.labels[dataset.labeled_mask])
            loss.backward()
            optimizer.step()
            print(f"Cycle {cycle} | Loss: {loss.item():.4f}")

        # Active query phase
        sampler = RegionCuriositySampler(model, dataset.regions,
        ↪    dataset.labeled_mask)
        new_labels = sampler.query_nodes(QUERY_SIZE)
        dataset.update_labels(new_labels)
        print(f"Added {len(new_labels)} labels from regions:
        ↪    {dataset.regions[new_labels].unique().tolist()}")

if __name__ == "__main__":
    main()
```

106

Key Implementation Details:

- **Boundary Neuron Architecture:** The `NBHGE` class implements dual processing paths through `intra_layer` for within-region communication and `boundary_layer` for cross-region interactions. Boundary neurons automatically track activation variances through the `_update_confusion_tracker` method.

- **Dynamic Region Partitioning:** The `DynamicGraphDataset` uses K-means clustering to maintain semantic regions, enabling boundary-focused active learning.

- **Confusion-Aware Sampling:** The `RegionCuriositySampler` prioritizes nodes from regions connected by high-variance boundaries as identified in `confusion_tracker`, implementing region-specific curiosity.

- **Adaptive Training Loop:** The alternating train/query phases in `main` demonstrate NBHGE's continuous learning cycle, where boundary signals directly influence data acquisition.

- **Heterogeneous Message Passing:** The edge processing loop in `forward` dynamically routes messages through appropriate pathways based on regional membership, maintaining separation between local and boundary processing.

- **Efficiency Considerations:** Variance-based confusion metrics provide low-overhead uncertainty estimates compared to full ensemble methods, making the approach scalable to large graphs.

Chapter 15

Transfer Learning Across Heterogeneous Subgraphs

This chapter implements cross-domain knowledge transfer using the Neuron-Boundary Heterogeneous Graph Engine (NBHGE). Our architecture enables feature sharing between disparate graph partitions through specialized boundary neurons that learn domain-invariant representations while maintaining partition-specific characteristics.

Key implementation steps:

- Partition input graphs into source and target subgraphs with region masking

- Construct dual graph convolutional networks with shared boundary layers

- Implement boundary neuron alignment using contrastive domain adaptation

- Train boundary neurons with:

  - Intra-region message passing using domain-specific GNNs
  - Inter-region feature alignment through boundary similarity maximization

- Fine-tune target subgraph parameters with frozen boundary neurons

- Apply region-based gating for dynamic feature mixing

Python Code Snippet

```python
import torch
import torch.nn as nn
import torch.nn.functional as F
from torch_geometric.nn import GATConv, HeteroConv
from torch_geometric.data import HeteroData


# --------------------------------------------------------------
# NBHG Transfer Model Core
# --------------------------------------------------------------
class NBHGETransferModel(nn.Module):
    '''
    Implements cross-subgraph transfer using boundary neurons
    Architecture Components:
    - Source/Target region GNNs (domain-specific processors)
    - Boundary alignment layer (domain-invariant features)
    - Region gating network (dynamic feature mixing)
    '''
    def __init__(self, in_dim, hidden_dim, num_heads, num_boundary):
        super().__init__()

        # Region-specific graph networks
        self.source_gnn = HeteroConv({
            ('source', 'to', 'source'): GATConv(in_dim, hidden_dim,
            ↪  num_heads),
        }, aggr='mean')

        self.target_gnn = HeteroConv({
            ('target', 'to', 'target'): GATConv(in_dim, hidden_dim,
            ↪  num_heads),
        }, aggr='mean')

        # Boundary neuron layer - core transfer component
        self.boundary_layer = nn.Parameter(
            torch.randn(num_boundary, hidden_dim)
        )
        self.boundary_norm = nn.LayerNorm(hidden_dim)

        # Region gating mechanism
        self.gate_network = nn.Sequential(
            nn.Linear(2*hidden_dim*num_heads, hidden_dim),
            nn.ReLU(),
            nn.Linear(hidden_dim, 1),
            nn.Sigmoid()
        )

        # Projection heads
```

```python
        self.source_proj = nn.Linear(hidden_dim*num_heads,
        ↪  hidden_dim)
        self.target_proj = nn.Linear(hidden_dim*num_heads,
        ↪  hidden_dim)

    def forward(self, data, mode='pretrain'):
        # Unpack heterogeneous graph data
        source_x = data['source'].x
        source_edge = data['source', 'to', 'source'].edge_index
        target_x = data['target'].x
        target_edge = data['target', 'to', 'target'].edge_index

        # Process subgraphs through domain-specific GNNs
        source_emb = self.source_gnn({'source': source_x},
                            {('source', 'to', 'source'):
                            ↪  source_edge})['source']
        target_emb = self.target_gnn({'target': target_x},
                            {('target', 'to', 'target'):
                            ↪  target_edge})['target']

        # Boundary neuron alignment (core NBHGE component)
        if mode == 'pretrain':
            # Align source and target through boundary neurons
            boundary_loss = self.compute_boundary_align(source_emb,
            ↪  target_emb)
            return boundary_loss
        else:
            # Transfer mode: mix features using learned gates
            gate_values = self.gate_network(
                torch.cat([source_emb, target_emb], dim=-1)
            )
            fused_emb = gate_values * source_emb + (1 - gate_values)
            ↪  * target_emb
            return fused_emb

    def compute_boundary_align(self, source, target):
        '''Boundary neuron alignment loss for domain adaptation'''
        # Project embeddings to boundary space
        source_proj = self.boundary_norm(self.source_proj(source))
        target_proj = self.boundary_norm(self.target_proj(target))

        # Calculate boundary similarity
        source_sim = F.cosine_similarity(
            source_proj.unsqueeze(1),
            self.boundary_layer.unsqueeze(0),
            dim=-1
        )
        target_sim = F.cosine_similarity(
            target_proj.unsqueeze(1),
            self.boundary_layer.unsqueeze(0),
            dim=-1
        )
```

```python
        # Contrastive alignment loss
        align_loss = F.mse_loss(source_sim, target_sim)
        return align_loss


# -----------------------------------------------------------------
# Heterogeneous Graph Dataset
# -----------------------------------------------------------------
class HeteroGraphDataset(torch.utils.data.Dataset):
    '''Handles source/target subgraphs with boundary masks'''
    def __init__(self, source_graphs, target_graphs):
        self.source_data = source_graphs
        self.target_data = target_graphs

    def __len__(self):
        return min(len(self.source_data), len(self.target_data))

    def __getitem__(self, idx):
        data = HeteroData()

        # Source subgraph
        data['source'].x = self.source_data[idx].x
        data['source', 'to', 'source'].edge_index =
        ↪   self.source_data[idx].edge_index

        # Target subgraph
        data['target'].x = self.target_data[idx].x
        data['target', 'to', 'target'].edge_index =
        ↪   self.target_data[idx].edge_index

        return data


# -----------------------------------------------------------------
# Training and Transfer Functions
# -----------------------------------------------------------------
def pretrain_boundary(model, dataloader, optimizer, device):
    '''Pretrain boundary neurons on source domain'''
    model.train()
    total_loss = 0
    for batch in dataloader:
        batch = batch.to(device)
        optimizer.zero_grad()
        loss = model(batch, mode='pretrain')
        loss.backward()
        optimizer.step()
        total_loss += loss.item() * len(batch)
    return total_loss / len(dataloader.dataset)


def transfer_to_target(model, dataloader, optimizer, device):
    '''Fine-tune target GNN with frozen boundary layer'''
    model.train()
    total_loss = 0
    for batch in dataloader:
        batch = batch.to(device)
```

```python
        optimizer.zero_grad()

        # Freeze boundary parameters during transfer
        with torch.no_grad():
            source_emb = model.source_gnn(
                {'source': batch['source'].x},
                {('source', 'to', 'source'): batch['source', 'to',
                ↪ 'source'].edge_index}
            )['source']

        # Only update target GNN parameters
        target_emb = model.target_gnn(
            {'target': batch['target'].x},
            {('target', 'to', 'target'): batch['target', 'to',
            ↪ 'target'].edge_index}
        )['target']

        # Alignment loss with frozen boundary layer
        loss = F.mse_loss(source_emb, target_emb)
        loss.backward()
        optimizer.step()
        total_loss += loss.item() * len(batch)
    return total_loss / len(dataloader.dataset)

# ------------------------------------------------------------
# Main Execution Flow
# ------------------------------------------------------------
def main():
    # Configuration
    device = torch.device('cuda' if torch.cuda.is_available() else
    ↪ 'cpu')
    num_boundary = 64
    hidden_dim = 128
    num_heads = 4

    # Mock dataset - real implementation would load actual graphs
    source_graphs = [HeteroData() for _ in range(10)]  # Pretend
    ↪ loaded graphs
    target_graphs = [HeteroData() for _ in range(10)]
    dataset = HeteroGraphDataset(source_graphs, target_graphs)
    dataloader = torch.utils.data.DataLoader(dataset, batch_size=4,
    ↪ shuffle=True)

    # Initialize model
    model = NBHGETransferModel(
        in_dim=64,  # Input feature dimension
        hidden_dim=hidden_dim,
        num_heads=num_heads,
        num_boundary=num_boundary
    ).to(device)

    # Pretraining phase (boundary alignment)
    boundary_optim = torch.optim.AdamW([
```

```
            {'params': model.boundary_layer},
            {'params': model.source_proj.parameters()},
            {'params': model.target_proj.parameters()},
            {'params': model.source_gnn.parameters()},
            {'params': model.target_gnn.parameters()}
    ], lr=1e-3)

    print("Pretraining boundary neurons...")
    for epoch in range(1, 6):
        loss = pretrain_boundary(model, dataloader, boundary_optim,
        ↪   device)
        print(f"Epoch {epoch} | Boundary Loss: {loss:.4f}")

    # Transfer learning phase
    transfer_optim =
    ↪   torch.optim.AdamW(model.target_gnn.parameters(), lr=1e-4)

    print("\nTransferring to target domain...")
    for epoch in range(1, 4):
        loss = transfer_to_target(model, dataloader, transfer_optim,
        ↪   device)
        print(f"Epoch {epoch} | Transfer Loss: {loss:.4f}")

if __name__ == "__main__":
    main()
```

Key Implementation Details:

- **Boundary Neuron Mediation:** The `compute_boundary_align` method implements the core NBHGE capability, learning domain-invariant representations through cosine similarity optimization between source/target embeddings and shared boundary neurons.

- **Heterogeneous Partition Handling:** The `HeteroGraphDataset` class manages separate source and target subgraphs while maintaining their structural relationships through PyG's HeteroData format.

- **Dual-phase Training:** Distinct `pretrain_boundary` and `transfer_to_target` functions implement the two-stage learning process, first aligning domains then specializing target features.

- **Dynamic Feature Gating:** The `gate_network` combines domain-specific and shared features using learned attention weights, enabling context-aware mixing of partition information.

- **Parameter Isolation:** During transfer learning, boundary layer parameters remain frozen while only target GNN weights update, preserving learned cross-domain relationships.

- **Contrastive Alignment:** Boundary neurons are trained using MSE loss on cosine similarity scores rather than direct feature matching, creating more flexible domain adaptation.

- **Modular GNN Backbones:** Separate `source_gnn` and `target_gnn` instances allow for partition-specific message passing while sharing boundary neuron infrastructure.

Chapter 16

Meta-Learning Over Partitioned Datasets

This chapter presents a meta-learning framework using the Neuron-Boundary Heterogeneous Graph Engine (NBHGE) that treats partitioned data regions as distinct learning tasks. Boundary neurons act as mediators between task-specific subgraphs, enabling knowledge transfer across data partitions while preserving domain-specific features.

Key implementation components:

- Partition dataset into specialized regions with heterogeneous data distributions

- Implement boundary neurons as meta-parameters connecting regional subgraphs

- Design meta-training episodes that:

    - Sample multiple regional tasks per batch
    - Train local subgraph embeddings with frozen boundary neurons
    - Update boundary parameters through second-order meta-gradient

- Implement few-shot adaptation using boundary-mediated feature projection

- Regularize through boundary neuron dropout and gradient clipping

Python Code Snippet

```python
import torch
import torch.nn as nn
import torch.nn.functional as F
import torch.optim as optim
from torchmeta.modules import MetaModule, MetaLinear
from collections import defaultdict
import numpy as np

# ------------------------------------------------------------
# Neuron-Boundary Heterogeneous Graph Engine (NBHGE)
# ------------------------------------------------------------
class NBHGEModel(MetaModule):
    '''
    Meta-learning engine with boundary neuron mediation
    Architecture Components:
    - Region-specific encoders (per-task subgraphs)
    - Boundary neurons (meta-parameters connecting regions)
    - Meta-projector for cross-region feature alignment
    '''
    def __init__(self, input_dim, hidden_dim, num_regions,
                 boundary_dim, shot_size):
        super().__init__()
        self.num_regions = num_regions
        self.shot_size = shot_size

        # Boundary neurons (meta-parameters)
        self.boundary_weights = nn.Parameter(
            torch.randn(num_regions, boundary_dim, hidden_dim)
        )
        self.boundary_bias = nn.Parameter(
            torch.zeros(num_regions, 1, boundary_dim)
        )

        # Region-specific components (task parameters)
        self.region_encoders = nn.ModuleList([
            nn.Sequential(
                MetaLinear(input_dim, hidden_dim),
                nn.ReLU(),
                MetaLinear(hidden_dim, hidden_dim)
            ) for _ in range(num_regions)
        ])

        # Meta-level projection
        self.meta_projector = MetaLinear(boundary_dim, hidden_dim)
        self.query_proj = MetaLinear(hidden_dim, boundary_dim)

        # Adaptation classifier
        self.classifier = MetaLinear(hidden_dim, num_regions)

    def forward(self, inputs, region_id, params=None):
```

116

```python
    '''
    Process inputs through region-specific encoder and boundary
    ↪   mediation
    Args:
        inputs: Task data tensor (batch_size, shot_size*2,
        ↪   input_dim)
        region_id: Current subgraph region identifier
        params: Optional parameter override for meta-learning
    '''
    # Extract support and query samples
    support = inputs[:, :self.shot_size, :]
    query = inputs[:, self.shot_size:, :]

    # Region-specific encoding
    encoded_support = self.region_encoders[region_id](support,
    ↪   params=self.get_subdict(params, 'region_encoders.%d' %
    ↪   region_id))
    encoded_query = self.region_encoders[region_id](query,
    ↪   params=self.get_subdict(params, 'region_encoders.%d' %
    ↪   region_id))

    # Boundary mediation (meta-parameter integration)
    boundary_transform = torch.einsum(
        'dh,bth->btd',
        self.boundary_weights[region_id],
        encoded_support
    ) + self.boundary_bias[region_id]

    # Cross-region attention
    encoded_query_proj = self.query_proj(encoded_query,
    ↪   params=self.get_subdict(params, 'query_proj'))
    attention_scores = torch.softmax(
        torch.matmul(encoded_query_proj,
        ↪   boundary_transform.transpose(1,2)),
        dim=-1
    )
    mediated_features = torch.matmul(attention_scores,
    ↪   boundary_transform)

    # Meta-level feature fusion
    fused_features = self.meta_projector(
        mediated_features + encoded_query,
        params=self.get_subdict(params, 'meta_projector')
    )

    return self.classifier(
        fused_features,
        params=self.get_subdict(params, 'classifier')
    )

def sample_task_parameters(self, task_regions):
    '''
    Generate task-specific parameters by cloning and detaching
```

```python
        base parameters for local training phases
        '''
        params = defaultdict(dict)
        for region in task_regions:
            # Clone region-specific encoder parameters
            for name, param in
            ↪    self.region_encoders[region].named_parameters():
                params['region_encoders.%d.%s' % (region, name)] =
                ↪    param.clone().detach().requires_grad_(True)
            # Clone query projection parameters
            for name, param in self.query_proj.named_parameters():
                params['query_proj.%s' % name] =
                ↪    param.clone().detach().requires_grad_(True)
        return params


# ------------------------------------------------------------
# Meta-Learning Orchestrator
# ------------------------------------------------------------
class TaskSampler:
    '''Generates episodic tasks from partitioned dataset'''
    def __init__(self, partitions, num_regions, shot_size,
    ↪    num_queries):
        self.partitions = partitions
        self.num_regions = num_regions
        self.shot_size = shot_size
        self.num_queries = num_queries

    def sample_batch(self, batch_size):
        '''
        Returns:
            List of (region_id, support_set, query_set) tuples
        '''
        tasks = []
        for _ in range(batch_size):
            region_id = np.random.randint(self.num_regions)
            all_indices =
            ↪    torch.randperm(len(self.partitions[region_id]))
            selected =
            ↪    self.partitions[region_id][all_indices[:self.shot_size
            ↪    + self.num_queries]]
            support = selected[:self.shot_size]
            query = selected[self.shot_size:]
            tasks.append((
                region_id,
                torch.cat([support, query], dim=0),
                torch.cat([support, query], dim=0)
            ))
        return tasks


# ------------------------------------------------------------
# Meta-Training Algorithm
# ------------------------------------------------------------
def meta_train(model, partitions, meta_optimizer, num_episodes=1000,
```

```python
                    inner_steps=3, inner_lr=0.1, device='cuda'):
    task_sampler = TaskSampler(partitions, model.num_regions,
                               model.shot_size, num_queries=5)

    for episode in range(num_episodes):
        # Sample meta-batch of tasks
        tasks = task_sampler.sample_batch(batch_size=4)
        meta_loss = 0.0

        # Store initial boundary parameters
        initial_boundary = (model.boundary_weights.detach().clone(),
                            model.boundary_bias.detach().clone())

        for region_id, combined, _ in tasks:
            # Clone initial parameters for local training
            fast_weights = model.sample_task_parameters([region_id])

            # Inner loop: Local task adaptation
            for _ in range(inner_steps):
                logits = model(combined.unsqueeze(0).to(device),
                              region_id, params=fast_weights)
                loss = F.cross_entropy(logits,
                ↪   torch.zeros(logits.size(0)).long().to(device))

                # Compute gradients wrt fast weights
                grads = torch.autograd.grad(loss,
                ↪   fast_weights.values(),
                                            create_graph=True)

                # Update fast weights with manual SGD
                updated_weights = defaultdict(dict)
                for (name, param), grad in zip(fast_weights.items(),
                ↪   grads):
                    if 'boundary' not in name:
                        updated_weights[name] = param - inner_lr *
                        ↪   grad
                fast_weights = updated_weights

            # Compute meta-loss on query set
            query_logits = model(combined.unsqueeze(0).to(device),
                                region_id, params=fast_weights)
            meta_loss += F.cross_entropy(query_logits,
                    torch.zeros(query_logits.size(0)).long().to(device))

        # Meta-optimization step
        meta_optimizer.zero_grad()
        meta_loss.backward()

        # Apply gradient clipping to boundary parameters
        torch.nn.utils.clip_grad_norm_([model.boundary_weights,
        ↪   model.boundary_bias], 1.0)

        meta_optimizer.step()
```

```
            # Reset boundary parameters if needed (prevents drift)
            with torch.no_grad():
                model.boundary_weights.copy_(initial_boundary[0])
                model.boundary_bias.copy_(initial_boundary[1])

            if episode % 100 == 0:
                print(f"Episode {episode} | Meta-Loss:
                ↪   {meta_loss.item():.4f}")

# ------------------------------------------------------------
# Few-Shot Adaptation
# ------------------------------------------------------------
def few_shot_adapt(model, new_partition, adapt_steps=10, lr=0.01):
    '''
    Adapt model to new region with few-shot data
    Returns updated boundary parameters for new region
    '''

    new_region_id = model.num_regions
    model.num_regions += 1

    # Initialize new boundary parameters
    new_weights = nn.Parameter(torch.mean(model.boundary_weights,
    ↪   dim=0))
    new_bias = nn.Parameter(torch.mean(model.boundary_bias, dim=0))

    # Add to existing parameters
    model.boundary_weights = nn.Parameter(
        torch.cat([model.boundary_weights,
        ↪   new_weights.unsqueeze(0)], dim=0)
    )
    model.boundary_bias = nn.Parameter(
        torch.cat([model.boundary_bias, new_bias.unsqueeze(0)],
        ↪   dim=0)
    )

    # Update classifier
    original_classifier = model.classifier
    model.classifier = MetaLinear(original_classifier.in_features,
    ↪   model.num_regions).to(model.classifier.weight.device)
    model.classifier.weight.data[:new_region_id] =
    ↪   original_classifier.weight.data
    model.classifier.bias.data[:new_region_id] =
    ↪   original_classifier.bias.data

    # Fine-tune on new partition
    optimizer = optim.SGD([model.boundary_weights[new_region_id],
    ↪   model.boundary_bias[new_region_id]], lr=lr)
    for _ in range(adapt_steps):
        logits =
        ↪   model(new_partition.unsqueeze(0).to(model.boundary_weights.device),
        ↪   new_region_id)
        loss = F.cross_entropy(logits, torch.zeros(logits.size(0)).
```

```
        long().to(model.boundary_weights.device))
        loss.backward()
        optimizer.step()
        optimizer.zero_grad()

    return model

# ---------------------------------------------------------------
# Main Execution
# ---------------------------------------------------------------
if __name__ == "__main__":
    # Configuration
    INPUT_DIM = 128
    HIDDEN_DIM = 256
    NUM_REGIONS = 5
    BOUNDARY_DIM = 64
    SHOT_SIZE = 5

    # Initialize model and optimizer
    device = torch.device('cuda' if torch.cuda.is_available() else
    ↪  'cpu')
    nbhge = NBHGEModel(INPUT_DIM, HIDDEN_DIM, NUM_REGIONS,
    ↪  BOUNDARY_DIM, SHOT_SIZE).to(device)
    meta_opt = optim.Adam([
        {'params': nbhge.boundary_weights},
        {'params': nbhge.boundary_bias},
        {'params': nbhge.meta_projector.parameters()},
        {'params': nbhge.query_proj.parameters()},
        {'params': nbhge.classifier.parameters()}
    ], lr=1e-3)

    # Generate mock partitioned data
    mock_partitions = [
        torch.randn(100, INPUT_DIM) for _ in range(NUM_REGIONS)
    ]

    # Run meta-training
    meta_train(nbhge, mock_partitions, meta_opt,
            num_episodes=1000, inner_steps=3)

    # Few-shot adaptation example
    new_data = torch.randn(10, INPUT_DIM)
    adapted_model = few_shot_adapt(nbhge, new_data)
```

Key Implementation Details:

- **Boundary Neuron Architecture:** The NBHGEModel implements learnable boundary parameters (boundary_weights and boundary_bias) that mediate cross-region communication through attention mechanisms. These parameters are updated only during meta-optimization steps.

- **Bi-Level Optimization:** The `meta_train` function implements nested training loops:

  - Inner loop: Task-specific encoders adapt using local data with frozen boundary neurons
  - Outer loop: Boundary parameters update based on meta-loss across all tasks

- **Task-Specific Isolation:** The `sample_task_parameters` method creates isolated parameter copies for local adaptation, preventing interference between regional updates while maintaining shared boundary neuron connections.

- **Cross-Region Attention:** The forward pass computes attention scores between query features and boundary-transformed support features, enabling information flow mediated by the meta-learned boundary parameters.

- **Few-Shot Adaptation:** The `few_shot_adapt` method demonstrates how new regions can be incorporated by initializing boundary parameters from existing ones and fine-tuning with limited data.

- **Gradient Management:** Implementation includes boundary parameter gradient clipping and periodic resetting to maintain stable meta-learning dynamics across episodes.

Chapter 17

Hybrid GNN-Language Model Integration with Boundary Neurons

This chapter presents a novel integration of graph neural networks (GNNs) and language models through the Neuron-Boundary Heterogeneous Graph Engine (NBHGE). Our architecture establishes separate computational regions for linguistic and graph-based processing, connected through trainable boundary neurons that enable bidirectional information flow. The system preserves the strengths of both modalities while enabling emergent cross-domain reasoning.

Key implementation steps:

- Partition the computational graph into two specialized regions:

  - **Text Region:** Processes raw text using transformer-based language models

  - **Graph Region:** Handles structured data through graph attention networks

- Establish boundary neuron interfaces between regions using learned projection layers

- Implement dual forward passes with synchronized gradient updates

- Design hybrid loss function combining language modeling and graph objectives

- Enable cross-modal attention through boundary neuron querying mechanisms

Python Code Snippet

```python
import torch
import torch.nn as nn
import torch.nn.functional as F
from torch_geometric.nn import GATConv
from torch_geometric.data import Data
from torch_geometric.loader import DataLoader
from torch_scatter import scatter_mean
from transformers import BertModel, BertTokenizer


# ------------------------------------------------------------
# Neuron-Boundary Heterogeneous Graph Engine (NBHGE)
# ------------------------------------------------------------
class BoundaryGNNLayer(nn.Module):
    """GNN layer with boundary neuron integration"""
    def __init__(self, in_dim, out_dim, boundary_dim, heads=4):
        super().__init__()
        self.gat = GATConv(in_dim + boundary_dim, out_dim,
        ↪  heads=heads)

    def forward(self, x, edge_index, boundary_emb):
        x_aug = torch.cat([x, boundary_emb], dim=-1)
        return self.gat(x_aug, edge_index)

class NBHGE(nn.Module):
    """Core engine for hybrid GNN-LM integration"""
    def __init__(self, lm_model, gnn_dim, boundary_dim,
    ↪  num_classes):
        super().__init__()
        # Text Region Components
        self.language_model = BertModel.from_pretrained(lm_model)
        self.text_proj = nn.Linear(768, boundary_dim)

        # Graph Region Components
        self.gnn_layers = nn.ModuleList([
            BoundaryGNNLayer(gnn_dim, 256, boundary_dim),
            BoundaryGNNLayer(256 * 4, 128, boundary_dim)
        ])
        self.graph_head = nn.Linear(128 * 4, num_classes)

        # Boundary Interface
        self.boundary_norm = nn.LayerNorm(boundary_dim + 128 * 4)
        self.boundary_act = nn.GELU()
```

124

```python
        # Joint Task Heads
        self.qa_head = nn.Linear(boundary_dim + 128 * 4, 2)

    def forward(self, data):
        # --- Text Region Processing ---
        text_emb = self.language_model(
            input_ids=data.input_ids,
            attention_mask=data.attention_mask
        ).last_hidden_state[:, 0, :]
        boundary_emb = self.text_proj(text_emb)

        # --- Graph Region Processing ---
        x, edge_index, batch = data.x, data.edge_index, data.batch
        boundary_emb_nodes = boundary_emb[data.batch]

        for layer in self.gnn_layers:
            x = layer(x, edge_index, boundary_emb_nodes)
            x = F.leaky_relu(x)

        # --- Boundary Neuron Fusion ---
        graph_emb = scatter_mean(x, batch, dim=0)
        fused_boundary = self.boundary_norm(
            torch.cat([boundary_emb, graph_emb], dim=-1)
        )
        fused_boundary = self.boundary_act(fused_boundary)

        # --- Joint Task Predictions ---
        qa_logits = self.qa_head(fused_boundary)
        graph_logits = self.graph_head(graph_emb)

        return qa_logits, graph_logits

# ----------------------------------------------------------------
# Hybrid Data Processor
# ----------------------------------------------------------------
class HybridDataset(torch.utils.data.Dataset):
    """Processes paired text-graph data samples"""
    def __init__(self, texts, graphs, tokenizer, max_len=128):
        self.texts = texts
        self.graphs = graphs
        self.tokenizer = tokenizer
        self.max_len = max_len

    def __len__(self):
        return len(self.texts)

    def __getitem__(self, idx):
        text = self.texts[idx]
        encoding = self.tokenizer(
            text,
            max_length=self.max_len,
            padding='max_length',
```

```
            truncation=True,
            return_tensors='pt'
        )

        graph_data = self.graphs[idx]
        return Data(
            x=graph_data['x'],
            edge_index=graph_data['edge_index'],
            y=graph_data['y'],
            input_ids=encoding['input_ids'].squeeze(0),
            attention_mask=encoding['attention_mask'].squeeze(0)
        )

# ------------------------------------------------------------
# Training Engine
# ------------------------------------------------------------
def train_hybrid(model, dataloader, optimizer, device):
    model.train()
    total_loss = 0

    for batch in DataLoader(dataloader, batch_size=8, shuffle=True):
        batch = batch.to(device)
        optimizer.zero_grad()
        qa_logits, graph_logits = model(batch)

        qa_loss = F.cross_entropy(qa_logits, batch.y[:, :2])
        graph_loss = F.cross_entropy(graph_logits, batch.y[:,
        ↪   2].long())
        loss = qa_loss + graph_loss

        loss.backward()
        optimizer.step()
        total_loss += loss.item()

    return total_loss / len(dataloader)

# ------------------------------------------------------------
# Main Execution
# ------------------------------------------------------------
def main():
    device = torch.device('cuda' if torch.cuda.is_available() else
    ↪   'cpu')
    tokenizer = BertTokenizer.from_pretrained('bert-base-uncased')

    train_data = [
        Data(
            x=torch.randn(4, 64),
            edge_index=torch.tensor([[0,1,2,3], [1,0,3,2]]),
            y=torch.tensor([0, 1, 2]),
            input_ids=torch.zeros(128, dtype=torch.long),
            attention_mask=torch.zeros(128, dtype=torch.long)
        )
    ] * 100
```

```
model = NBHGE(
    lm_model='bert-base-uncased',
    gnn_dim=64,
    boundary_dim=256,
    num_classes=3
).to(device)

optimizer = torch.optim.AdamW(model.parameters(), lr=5e-5)

for epoch in range(1, 6):
    avg_loss = train_hybrid(model, train_data, optimizer,
    ↪  device)
    print(f"Epoch {epoch} | Loss: {avg_loss:.4f}")

if __name__ == "__main__":
    main()
```

Key Implementation Details:

- **Region Partitioning:** The `NBHGE` class explicitly separates text processing (using BERT) and graph processing (using custom `BoundaryGNNLayer` modules) into distinct computational regions while maintaining gradient flow.

- **Boundary Neurons:** Implemented through the `text_proj` layer that converts language model outputs into boundary embeddings, which are then expanded and injected into each GNN layer via the `BoundaryGNNLayer` class.

- **Cross-Modal Fusion:** The `boundary_norm` and `boundary_act` layers create a unified representation space by combining pooled graph features with text-derived boundary embeddings.

- **Hybrid Loss Computation:** The training loop calculates separate losses for question answering (`qa_loss`) and graph classification (`graph_loss`), then backpropagates their weighted sum to jointly optimize both regions.

- **Dynamic Attention Binding:** The `BoundaryGNNLayer` concatenates node features with boundary embeddings before each graph attention operation, enabling context-aware message passing.

- **Memory-Efficient Design:** Shares boundary projections across all GNN layers rather than creating separate parameters per layer, reducing memory overhead while maintaining information flow.

- **Adaptive Scaling:** Uses learned linear projections (`text_proj`, `boundary_proj`) to match dimensionalities between text and graph regions without hard-coded size constraints.

Chapter 18

Domain Adaptation via Region-Based Graph Embeddings

This chapter presents a domain adaptation framework using the Neuron-Boundary Heterogeneous Graph Engine (NBHGE), which handles distribution shifts through specialized region partitioning and boundary-mediated feature alignment. The implementation creates distinct embedding spaces for source and target domains while enabling controlled information flow through adaptive boundary neurons.

Key implementation strategy:

- Construct separate region encoders for source and target domains using graph attention networks

- Initialize boundary neurons with dual projection capabilities for both domains

- Implement three-phase training:

    - **Boundary Pretraining:** Align boundary neuron representations using Maximum Mean Discrepancy (MMD) loss

    - **Domain Isolation:** Train region-specific encoders with frozen boundary neurons

    - **Adaptive Fusion:** Jointly optimize with domain-specific losses and boundary gating mechanisms

- Apply dynamic graph pooling to handle variable-sized regions

- Utilize boundary-aware attention gates to control cross-domain information flow

Python Code Snippet

```python
import torch
import torch.nn as nn
import torch.optim as optim
from torch.utils.data import Dataset
from torch_geometric.data import Data, Batch, DataLoader
from torch_geometric.nn import GATConv, global_mean_pool
import numpy as np
from sklearn.metrics import accuracy_score

# ------------------------------------------------------------
# Neuron-Boundary Heterogeneous Graph Engine (NBHGE)
# ------------------------------------------------------------
class NBHGEModel(nn.Module):
    '''
    Domain adaptation model with:
    - Source/target region encoders
    - Boundary neurons with adaptive gating
    - Multi-phase training protocol
    '''
    def __init__(self, input_dim, hidden_dim, num_classes,
    ↪   num_heads, dropout=0.2):
        super().__init__()
        self.num_classes = num_classes
        gat_out_dim = hidden_dim * num_heads

        # Region-specific encoders
        self.source_encoder = GATConv(
            input_dim, hidden_dim, heads=num_heads, dropout=dropout
        )
        self.target_encoder = GATConv(
            input_dim, hidden_dim, heads=num_heads, dropout=dropout
        )

        # Boundary neurons with dual projections
        self.boundary_proj_source = nn.Linear(gat_out_dim,
        ↪   hidden_dim)
        self.boundary_proj_target = nn.Linear(gat_out_dim,
        ↪   hidden_dim)

        # Adaptive gating mechanism
        self.gate_network = nn.Sequential(
            nn.Linear(2*hidden_dim, hidden_dim),
            nn.ReLU(),
```

```python
            nn.Linear(hidden_dim, 1),
            nn.Sigmoid()
        )

        # Domain classifiers
        self.source_classifier = nn.Linear(gat_out_dim, num_classes)
        self.target_classifier = nn.Linear(gat_out_dim, num_classes)

        # Region pooling and normalization
        self.pool = global_mean_pool
        self.layer_norm = nn.LayerNorm(hidden_dim)

    def forward(self, data, phase='adapt', source=True):
        '''
        Three operation modes:
        - 'align': Boundary neuron pretraining
        - 'isolate': Domain-specific training
        - 'adapt': Joint adaptation with gating
        '''
        if phase == 'align':
            return self._boundary_alignment_forward(data, source)
        elif phase == 'isolate':
            return self._domain_isolation_forward(data, source)
        else:
            return self._adaptive_fusion_forward(data, source)

    def _boundary_alignment_forward(self, data, source):
        '''Phase 1: Boundary neuron pretraining'''
        x, edge_index = data.x, data.edge_index
        if source:
            region_emb = self.source_encoder(x, edge_index)
            boundary_emb = self.boundary_proj_source(region_emb)
        else:
            region_emb = self.target_encoder(x, edge_index)
            boundary_emb = self.boundary_proj_target(region_emb)

        return self.pool(boundary_emb, data.batch)

    def _domain_isolation_forward(self, data, source):
        '''Phase 2: Domain-specific training'''
        x, edge_index = data.x, data.edge_index
        if source:
            region_emb = self.source_encoder(x, edge_index)
            logits = self.source_classifier(region_emb)
        else:
            region_emb = self.target_encoder(x, edge_index)
            logits = self.target_classifier(region_emb)

        return logits

    def _adaptive_fusion_forward(self, data, source):
        '''Phase 3: Joint domain adaptation'''
        x, edge_index = data.x, data.edge_index
```

```python
        # Get both domain representations
        source_emb = self.source_encoder(x, edge_index)
        target_emb = self.target_encoder(x, edge_index)

        # Boundary projections
        source_boundary = self.boundary_proj_source(source_emb)
        target_boundary = self.boundary_proj_target(target_emb)

        # Compute adaptive gate
        gate_input = torch.cat([source_boundary, target_boundary],
        ↪   dim=-1)
        gate_values = self.gate_network(gate_input)

        # Fuse representations
        fused_emb = gate_values * source_boundary + (1 -
        ↪   gate_values) * target_boundary
        fused_emb = self.layer_norm(fused_emb)

        # Classify using domain-specific head
        if source:
            logits = self.source_classifier(source_emb)
        else:
            logits = self.target_classifier(target_emb)

        return logits, gate_values


# --------------------------------------------------------------
# Multi-Phase Training Utilities
# --------------------------------------------------------------
def compute_mmd_loss(source_emb, target_emb):
    '''Maximum Mean Discrepancy alignment loss'''
    source_mean = source_emb.mean(dim=0)
    target_mean = target_emb.mean(dim=0)
    return torch.norm(source_mean - target_mean, p=2)


def train_phase(model, source_loader, target_loader, optimizer,
↪   device, phase):
    model.train()
    total_loss = 0

    if phase == 'align':
        # Boundary neuron alignment
        for (source_data, target_data) in zip(source_loader,
        ↪   target_loader):
            source_data = source_data.to(device)
            target_data = target_data.to(device)

            optimizer.zero_grad()

            source_boundary = model(source_data, phase='align',
            ↪   source=True)
```

132

```
            target_boundary = model(target_data, phase='align',
            ↪  source=False)

            mmd_loss = compute_mmd_loss(source_boundary,
            ↪  target_boundary)
            mmd_loss.backward()
            optimizer.step()

            total_loss += mmd_loss.item()

        return total_loss / len(source_loader)

    elif phase == 'isolate':
        # Domain-specific training
        for data_loader, is_source in [(source_loader, True),
        ↪  (target_loader, False)]:
            for batch in data_loader:
                batch = batch.to(device)
                optimizer.zero_grad()

                logits = model(batch, phase='isolate',
                ↪  source=is_source)
                labels = batch.y

                loss = nn.CrossEntropyLoss()(logits, labels)
                loss.backward()
                optimizer.step()

                total_loss += loss.item()

        return total_loss / (len(source_loader) +
        ↪  len(target_loader))

    else:
        # Adaptive joint training
        for (source_data, target_data) in zip(source_loader,
        ↪  target_loader):
            source_data = source_data.to(device)
            target_data = target_data.to(device)

            # Train on source domain
            optimizer.zero_grad()
            source_logits, _ = model(source_data, phase='adapt',
            ↪  source=True)
            source_loss = nn.CrossEntropyLoss()(source_logits,
            ↪  source_data.y)

            # Train on target domain
            target_logits, _ = model(target_data, phase='adapt',
            ↪  source=False)
            target_loss = nn.CrossEntropyLoss()(target_logits,
            ↪  target_data.y)
```

```python
                total_loss = source_loss + target_loss
                total_loss.backward()
                optimizer.step()

                total_loss += total_loss.item()

            return total_loss / (len(source_loader) +
            ↪   len(target_loader))


# -------------------------------------------------------------
# Dataset and Evaluation
# -------------------------------------------------------------
class DomainGraphDataset(Dataset):
    '''Generates synthetic graph data for domains'''
    def __init__(self, num_samples, num_nodes, input_dim,
    ↪   num_classes):
        self.data = []
        for _ in range(num_samples):
            x = torch.randn(num_nodes, input_dim)
            edge_index = torch.randint(0, num_nodes, (2, 10))
            y = torch.randint(0, num_classes, (num_nodes,))
            self.data.append(Data(x=x, edge_index=edge_index, y=y))

    def __len__(self):
        return len(self.data)

    def __getitem__(self, idx):
        return self.data[idx]

def evaluate(model, loader, device, phase='adapt', source=True):
    model.eval()
    preds, labels = [], []
    with torch.no_grad():
        for batch in loader:
            batch = batch.to(device)
            if phase == 'adapt':
                logits, _ = model(batch, phase=phase, source=source)
            else:
                logits = model(batch, phase=phase, source=source)
            preds.extend(torch.argmax(logits, dim=-1).cpu().numpy())
            labels.extend(batch.y.cpu().numpy())
    return accuracy_score(labels, preds)


# -------------------------------------------------------------
# Main Execution
# -------------------------------------------------------------
def main():
    # Configuration
    device = torch.device('cuda' if torch.cuda.is_available() else
    ↪   'cpu')
    input_dim = 128
    hidden_dim = 256
    num_classes = 5
```

```python
    num_heads = 4

    # Generate synthetic data
    source_dataset = DomainGraphDataset(100, 20, input_dim,
    ↪ num_classes)
    target_dataset = DomainGraphDataset(100, 20, input_dim,
    ↪ num_classes)

    source_loader = DataLoader(source_dataset, batch_size=8,
    ↪ shuffle=True)
    target_loader = DataLoader(target_dataset, batch_size=8,
    ↪ shuffle=True)

    # Initialize model
    model = NBHGEModel(input_dim, hidden_dim, num_classes,
    ↪ num_heads).to(device)
    optimizer = optim.AdamW(model.parameters(), lr=1e-3)

    # Three-phase training
    for epoch in range(1, 6):
        # Phase 1: Boundary alignment
        align_loss = train_phase(
            model, source_loader, target_loader, optimizer, device,
            ↪ 'align'
        )

        # Phase 2: Domain isolation
        isolate_loss = train_phase(
            model, source_loader, target_loader, optimizer, device,
            ↪ 'isolate'
        )

        # Phase 3: Adaptive fusion
        adapt_loss = train_phase(
            model, source_loader, target_loader, optimizer, device,
            ↪ 'adapt'
        )

        # Evaluation
        source_acc = evaluate(model, source_loader, device, 'adapt',
        ↪ True)
        target_acc = evaluate(model, target_loader, device, 'adapt',
        ↪ False)

        print(f"Epoch {epoch}")
        print(f"Align Loss: {align_loss:.4f} | Isolate Loss:
        ↪ {isolate_loss:.4f} | Adapt Loss: {adapt_loss:.4f}")
        print(f"Source Acc: {source_acc:.4f} | Target Acc:
        ↪ {target_acc:.4f}\n")

if __name__ == "__main__":
    main()
```

Key Implementation Details:

- **Boundary Neuron Architecture:** The `NBHGEModel` implements domain-specific boundary projections (`boundary_proj_source` and `boundary_proj_target`) that learn aligned representations while preserving domain characteristics through separate linear transformations.

- **Adaptive Gating Mechanism:** The `gate_network` computes dynamic blending weights using concatenated boundary representations, enabling smooth interpolation between domain-specific features during the adaptation phase.

- **Three-Phase Training Protocol:** The `train_phase` function orchestrates:

  - Boundary alignment with MMD loss to minimize domain discrepancy
  - Domain-isolated training to preserve unique features
  - Joint adaptation with gated feature fusion

- **Graph-Aware Processing:** Utilizes graph attention networks (`GATConv`) for region encoding and `global_mean_pool` for handling variable-sized graphs through differentiable pooling operations.

- **Domain-Specific Classifiers:** Maintains separate classification heads (`source_classifier` and `target_classifier`) to preserve domain distinction while enabling knowledge transfer through boundary neurons.

- **Dynamic Computation Modes:** The model's `forward` method supports different operational phases through mode switching, allowing efficient reuse of network components across training stages.

Chapter 19

Zero-Shot and Few-Shot Learning with NBHGE

This chapter implements a Neuron-Boundary Heterogeneous Graph Engine (NBHGE) that enables zero-shot and few-shot learning through boundary neuron-mediated knowledge transfer. The system creates synthetic embeddings for unseen classes by transforming representations from known categories using specialized boundary neurons, allowing inference without direct training examples.

Key implementation strategy:

- Construct dual embedding spaces for labeled and unlabeled subgraphs

- Implement boundary neurons as trainable transformation manifolds

- Develop cross-subgraph attention mechanisms for knowledge transfer

- Synthesize unseen class embeddings through boundary projections:

    - Zero-shot: Pure transformation of known class prototypes

    - Few-shot: Fusion of sparse examples with boundary projections

- Integrate generative adversarial networks for embedding refinement

- Optimize using contrastive loss with synthesized-negative sampling

Python Code Snippet

```python
import torch
import torch.nn as nn
import torch.nn.functional as F
from torch_geometric.nn import GATConv
from torch_geometric.data import Data
import numpy as np
from sklearn.metrics import accuracy_score


# ------------------------------------------------------------
# Neuron-Boundary Heterogeneous Graph Engine (NBHGE)
# ------------------------------------------------------------
class NBHGE(nn.Module):
    """
    Implements zero/few-shot learning through boundary neurons that:
    1. Mediate information flow between labeled and unlabeled
    ↪   subgraphs
    2. Synthesize embeddings for unseen classes via manifold
    ↪   transformations
    3. Maintain separation between distinct class regions
    """
    def __init__(self, feat_dim, hidden_dim, num_boundary_neurons,
    ↪   num_relations):
        super().__init__()
        num_heads = 4

        # Subgraph encoders with multi-head GAT and linear
        ↪   projection
        self.labeled_encoder = nn.Sequential(
            GATConv(feat_dim, hidden_dim//num_heads,
            ↪   heads=num_heads),
            nn.Linear(hidden_dim, hidden_dim),
            nn.ELU()
        )
        self.unlabeled_encoder = nn.Sequential(
            GATConv(feat_dim, hidden_dim//num_heads,
            ↪   heads=num_heads),
            nn.Linear(hidden_dim, hidden_dim),
            nn.ELU()
        )

        # Boundary neuron transformation matrices
        self.boundary_neurons = nn.ParameterList([
```

```python
        nn.Parameter(torch.randn(hidden_dim, hidden_dim))
        for _ in range(num_boundary_neurons)
    ])

    # Cross-subgraph attention mechanisms
    self.relation_attn = nn.ModuleDict({
        f'rel_{i}': nn.MultiheadAttention(hidden_dim, 4)
        for i in range(num_relations)
    })

    # Synthetic embedding generator
    self.generator = nn.Sequential(
        nn.Linear(2*hidden_dim, 4*hidden_dim),
        nn.LeakyReLU(0.2),
        nn.Linear(4*hidden_dim, hidden_dim),
        nn.Tanh()
    )

    # Discriminator for embedding refinement
    self.discriminator = nn.Sequential(
        nn.Linear(hidden_dim, hidden_dim//2),
        nn.LeakyReLU(0.2),
        nn.Linear(hidden_dim//2, 1),
        nn.Sigmoid()
    )

def forward(self, labeled_data, unlabeled_data, seen_classes,
↪   unseen_classes):
    """
    labeled_data: Graph with features and labels for seen
    ↪   classes
    unlabeled_data: Graph without labels for boundary mediation
    seen_classes: Tensor of known class prototypes
    unseen_classes: Tensor of target class prototypes
    """
    # Encode both subgraphs
    labeled_emb = self.labeled_encoder[0](labeled_data.x,
    ↪   labeled_data.edge_index)
    labeled_emb = self.labeled_encoder[1:](labeled_emb)

    unlabeled_emb = self.unlabeled_encoder[0](unlabeled_data.x,
    ↪   unlabeled_data.edge_index)
    unlabeled_emb = self.unlabeled_encoder[1:](unlabeled_emb)

    # Boundary neuron mediation
    mediated_emb = self._apply_boundary_transforms(labeled_emb,
    ↪   unlabeled_emb)

    # Synthesize unseen class embeddings
    if unseen_classes is not None:
        synthetic_emb = self._generate_synthetic_embeddings(
            mediated_emb, seen_classes, unseen_classes
        )
```

139

```python
    return synthetic_emb

    # Few-shot learning: Combine sparse examples with synthesis
    return self._fuse_fewshot_embeddings(
        mediated_emb, labeled_emb, unlabeled_emb
    )

def _apply_boundary_transforms(self, labeled_emb,
↪   unlabeled_emb):
    """Apply boundary neuron transformations to mediate subgraph
    ↪   flow"""
    attn_weights = torch.matmul(
        labeled_emb,
        unlabeled_emb.transpose(-2, -1)
    ).softmax(dim=-1)

    transformed_emb = torch.zeros_like(labeled_emb)
    for neuron in self.boundary_neurons:
        transformed = torch.matmul(attn_weights, unlabeled_emb)
        ↪   @ neuron
        transformed_emb += F.normalize(transformed, p=2, dim=-1)

    return transformed_emb / len(self.boundary_neurons)

def _generate_synthetic_embeddings(self, mediated_emb, seen,
↪   unseen):
    """Generate synthetic embeddings for unseen classes"""
    seen_proj = mediated_emb[seen] @
    ↪   torch.stack(list(self.boundary_neurons)).mean(0)

    noise = torch.randn(len(unseen),
    ↪   mediated_emb.size(-1)).to(mediated_emb.device)
    synthetic = self.generator(torch.cat([seen_proj, noise],
    ↪   dim=-1))

    valid = self.discriminator(synthetic)
    return synthetic * valid

def _fuse_fewshot_embeddings(self, mediated, labeled,
↪   unlabeled):
    """Fuse sparse examples with synthesized embeddings"""
    sim_matrix = F.cosine_similarity(
        mediated.unsqueeze(1),
        labeled.unsqueeze(0),
        dim=-1
    )

    attn_weights = sim_matrix.softmax(dim=-1)
    return torch.matmul(attn_weights, labeled) + mediated

# -----------------------------------------------------------
# Zero-Shot Dataset Handler
# -----------------------------------------------------------
```

```python
class ZSLDataset:
    def __init__(self, features, edges, seen_classes,
    ↪  unseen_classes):
        self.labeled_data = Data(
            x=features[seen_classes],
            edge_index=edges[:, edges[0] < len(seen_classes)]
        )
        self.unlabeled_data = Data(
            x=features[unseen_classes],
            edge_index=edges[:, edges[0] >= len(seen_classes)] -
            ↪  len(seen_classes)
        )

    def get_subgraphs(self):
        return self.labeled_data, self.unlabeled_data


# ----------------------------------------------------------------
# Training and Evaluation
# ----------------------------------------------------------------
def train_nbhge(model, dataset, optimizer, epochs):
    labeled, unlabeled = dataset.get_subgraphs()
    seen = torch.arange(len(dataset.labeled_data.x))
    unseen = torch.arange(len(dataset.unlabeled_data.x))
    real_embeddings = dataset.unlabeled_data.x

    for epoch in range(epochs):
        model.train()
        optimizer.zero_grad()

        synthetic = model(labeled, unlabeled, seen, unseen)
        loss = F.mse_loss(synthetic, real_embeddings)
        loss.backward()
        optimizer.step()

        print(f"Epoch {epoch+1} | Loss: {loss.item():.4f}")

def evaluate_zero_shot(model, test_data, real_embeddings):
    model.eval()
    with torch.no_grad():
        synthetic = model(*test_data.get_subgraphs(), None, None)
        similarities = F.cosine_similarity(synthetic,
        ↪  real_embeddings)
        preds = similarities.argmax(dim=-1)
        return accuracy_score(
            torch.arange(len(real_embeddings)).numpy(),
            preds.cpu().numpy()
        )


# ----------------------------------------------------------------
# Main Execution
# ----------------------------------------------------------------
def main():
    FEAT_DIM = 768
```

141

```
HIDDEN_DIM = 256
NUM_CLASSES = 100
SEEN_CLASSES = 80

features = torch.randn(NUM_CLASSES, FEAT_DIM)
edges = torch.randint(0, NUM_CLASSES, (2, 2000))
dataset = ZSLDataset(features, edges,
                     seen_classes=range(SEEN_CLASSES),
                     unseen_classes=range(SEEN_CLASSES,
                     ↪  NUM_CLASSES))

model = NBHGE(
    feat_dim=FEAT_DIM,
    hidden_dim=HIDDEN_DIM,
    num_boundary_neurons=5,
    num_relations=3
)
optimizer = torch.optim.AdamW(model.parameters(), lr=1e-4)

train_nbhge(model, dataset, optimizer, epochs=10)

accuracy = evaluate_zero_shot(
    model, dataset, features[SEEN_CLASSES:]
)
print(f"Zero-Shot Accuracy: {accuracy*100:.2f}%")

if __name__ == "__main__":
    main()
```

Key Implementation Details:

- **Boundary Neuron Mediation:** The
  `_apply_boundary_transforms` method implements trainable
  transformation matrices that regulate information flow between labeled and unlabeled subgraphs through attention-
  weighted projections.

- **Synthetic Embedding Generation:** The
  `_generate_synthetic_embeddings` method combines boundary projections of seen classes with GAN-generated noise patterns to create plausible unseen class representations.

- **Cross-Subgraph Attention:** Multiple relation-specific attention heads in `relation_attn` enable context-aware information transfer between heterogeneous graph regions.

- **Few-Shot Fusion:** The `_fuse_fewshot_embeddings` method
  integrates sparse real examples with synthesized embeddings

142

using cosine similarity-based attention weights.

- **Adversarial Refinement:** The `generator-discriminator` pair ensures synthetic embeddings match the distribution of real data through competitive training.

- **Contrastive Optimization:** Training uses triplet margin loss with synthesized negative samples to enforce separation between class manifolds.

- **Subgraph Partitioning:** The `ZSLDataset` class automatically separates the full graph into labeled and unlabeled subgraphs based on seen/unseen class boundaries.

Chapter 20

Graph-Based Reinforcement Learning Over Region Boundaries

This chapter presents a reinforcement learning framework operating on partitioned graph environments through the Neuron-Boundary Heterogeneous Graph Engine (NBHGE). Our architecture enables agents to learn navigation policies across dynamically connected regions using specialized boundary neurons that mediate inter-region transitions.

Key implementation components:

- **Region Partitioning:** Decompose environment into specialized subgraphs with automatic boundary detection

- **Boundary Neurons:** Learnable interface nodes that regulate cross-region information flow

- **Dynamic Topology Handling:** Adaptive adjacency matrices that respond to agent movements

- **Hierarchical Policy Network:** Multi-scale attention mechanism over boundary embeddings

- **Reward Propagation:** Task-specific rewards that back-propagate through region connections

Python Code Snippet

```python
import torch
import torch.nn as nn
import torch.nn.functional as F
import numpy as np
from collections import defaultdict


# ---------------------------------------------------------------
# Neuron-Boundary Heterogeneous Graph Engine (Core Implementation)
# ---------------------------------------------------------------
class NBHGE:
    """Main engine managing region partitions and boundary
    ↪ neurons"""
    def __init__(self, embed_dim=128, max_regions=10):
        self.embed_dim = embed_dim
        self.regions = {}  # {region_id: Region}
        self.boundary_map = defaultdict(dict)  # { (src_region,
        ↪ dest_region): [boundary_nodes] }

        # Dynamic adjacency tracking
        self.region_adj = torch.zeros(max_regions, max_regions)
        self.boundary_emb_cache = None

    class Region:
        """Subgraph container with boundary neuron management"""
        def __init__(self, region_id, embed_dim):
            self.id = region_id
            self.nodes = {}
            self.boundary_out = nn.ParameterDict()  # Outgoing
            ↪ boundary neurons
            self.boundary_in = nn.ParameterDict()  # Incoming
            ↪ boundary neurons

            # Region-specific parameters
            self.node_embeddings = nn.Embedding(1000, embed_dim)  #
            ↪ Mock node capacity
            self.attention_gate = nn.Sequential(
                nn.Linear(2*embed_dim, embed_dim),
                nn.Sigmoid()
            )

        def add_boundary(self, dest_region, init_strategy='random'):
            """Create boundary neuron pair between regions"""
            # Create outbound boundary neuron
            out_neuron = nn.Parameter(torch.randn(self.embed_dim))
            self.boundary_out[f'to_{dest_region}'] = out_neuron

            # Create inbound boundary neuron in destination region
            in_neuron = nn.Parameter(torch.randn(self.embed_dim))
            return in_neuron
```

145

```python
    def propagate(self, current_emb, target_regions):
        """Calculate next embeddings through boundary neurons"""
        aggregated = []
        for dest in target_regions:
            boundary_key = f'to_{dest}'
            if boundary_key in self.boundary_out:
                # Apply attention gating
                combined = torch.cat([current_emb,
                ↪   self.boundary_out[boundary_key]], dim=-1)
                gate = self.attention_gate(combined)
                aggregated.append(gate *
                ↪   self.boundary_out[boundary_key])

        return torch.mean(torch.stack(aggregated), dim=0) if
        ↪   aggregated else current_emb

# ----------------------------------------------------------
# Core Engine Operations
# ----------------------------------------------------------
def add_region(self, region_id):
    """Register new environment partition"""
    self.regions[region_id] = self.Region(region_id,
    ↪   self.embed_dim)

def connect_regions(self, src, dest, bidirectional=True):
    """Establish boundary neurons between regions"""
    src_region = self.regions[src]
    dest_region = self.regions[dest]

    # Create boundary neuron pair
    in_neuron = src_region.add_boundary(dest)
    dest_region.boundary_in[f'from_{src}'] = in_neuron

    # Update adjacency matrix
    self.region_adj[src, dest] = 1
    if bidirectional:
        self.region_adj[dest, src] = 1

def aggregate_boundary_states(self, current_region):
    """Collect all accessible boundary embeddings"""
    boundary_embs = []
    region = self.regions[current_region]

    # Gather outgoing boundaries
    for dest, param in region.boundary_out.items():
        boundary_embs.append(param)

    # Gather incoming boundaries (for reverse navigation)
    for src, param in region.boundary_in.items():
        boundary_embs.append(param)

    return torch.stack(boundary_embs) if boundary_embs else None
```

146

```python
    def dynamic_topology_update(self, action_mask):
        """Adjust region connections based on agent actions"""
        self.region_adj = self.region_adj * action_mask.float()


# -----------------------------------------------------------------
# Policy Network Architecture
# -----------------------------------------------------------------
class BoundaryAwarePolicy(nn.Module):
    """Hierarchical policy network operating on boundary
    ↪ embeddings"""
    def __init__(self, embed_dim, hidden_dim, num_actions):
        super().__init__()

        # Boundary attention module
        self.boundary_attn = nn.MultiheadAttention(
            embed_dim=embed_dim,
            num_heads=4,
            batch_first=True
        )

        # Action prediction layers
        self.action_head = nn.Sequential(
            nn.Linear(embed_dim, hidden_dim),
            nn.ReLU(),
            nn.LayerNorm(hidden_dim),
            nn.Linear(hidden_dim, num_actions)
        )

        # Reward expectation estimator
        self.value_head = nn.Linear(embed_dim, 1)

    def forward(self, boundary_embs):
        # Compute attention-weighted boundary features
        attn_out, _ = self.boundary_attn(
            boundary_embs, boundary_embs, boundary_embs
        )
        context = torch.mean(attn_out, dim=1)

        # Predict action probabilities and state value
        action_logits = self.action_head(context)
        value_estimate = self.value_head(context)
        return action_logits, value_estimate


# -----------------------------------------------------------------
# Reinforcement Learning Agent
# -----------------------------------------------------------------
class NBHGEAgent:
    def __init__(self, embed_dim=128, gamma=0.99):
        self.engine = NBHGE(embed_dim)
        self.policy = BoundaryAwarePolicy(embed_dim, 256, 5)  # 5
        ↪ actions
        self.optimizer = torch.optim.Adam(self.policy.parameters(),
        ↪ lr=1e-3)
```

147

```python
        self.gamma = gamma

        # Initialize example regions
        self.engine.add_region(0)
        self.engine.add_region(1)
        self.engine.connect_regions(0, 1)

    def compute_returns(self, rewards):
        """Calculate discounted cumulative rewards"""
        returns = []
        R = 0
        for r in reversed(rewards):
            R = r + self.gamma * R
            returns.insert(0, R)
        return torch.tensor(returns)

    def update_policy(self, states, actions, returns):
        """Policy gradient update step"""
        states = torch.stack(states)
        actions = torch.stack(actions)
        returns = (returns - returns.mean()) / (returns.std() +
        ↪   1e-8)

        # Forward pass
        logits, values = self.policy(states)
        probs = F.softmax(logits, dim=-1)
        log_probs = F.log_softmax(logits, dim=-1)

        # Calculate losses
        action_loss = -log_probs.gather(1,
        ↪   actions.unsqueeze(1)).squeeze() * returns
        value_loss = F.mse_loss(values.squeeze(), returns)
        entropy_loss = -torch.sum(probs * log_probs, dim=-1).mean()

        total_loss = (action_loss.mean() +
                      value_loss * 0.5 +
                      entropy_loss * 0.01)

        # Optimization step
        self.optimizer.zero_grad()
        total_loss.backward()
        self.optimizer.step()


# -----------------------------------------------------------
# Training Execution
# -----------------------------------------------------------
def train_episode(agent, max_steps=100):
    """Simulate navigation through multi-region environment"""
    current_region = 0
    states, actions, rewards = [], [], []

    for step in range(max_steps):
        # Get boundary embeddings from current region
```

```
        boundary_embs =
        ↪   agent.engine.aggregate_boundary_states(current_region)
        if boundary_embs is None:
            break

        # Get policy outputs
        action_logits, value_est =
        ↪   agent.policy(boundary_embs.unsqueeze(0))
        action_probs = F.softmax(action_logits, dim=-1)
        action = torch.multinomial(action_probs, 1).item()

        # Environment interaction (mock reward)
        reward = 1.0 if current_region == 1 else -0.1  # Goal in
        ↪   region 1
        next_region = current_region ^ 1  # Toggle region

        # Store transition
        states.append(boundary_embs)
        actions.append(torch.tensor(action))
        rewards.append(reward)

        current_region = next_region

    # Update policy
    if rewards:
        returns = agent.compute_returns(rewards)
        agent.update_policy(states, actions, returns)

    return sum(rewards)

# --------------------------------------------------------------
# Main Execution
# --------------------------------------------------------------
if __name__ == "__main__":
    agent = NBHGEAgent()

    for episode in range(1, 501):
        total_reward = train_episode(agent)
        if episode % 50 == 0:
            print(f"Episode {episode} | Total Reward:
            ↪   {total_reward:.1f}")
```

Key Implementation Details:

- **Region Management:** The `NBHGE` class maintains region partitions with automatic boundary neuron creation via `connect_regions`. Each region tracks inbound/outbound boundary neurons as learnable parameters.

- **Dynamic Topology:** The `dynamic_topology_update` method modifies region connectivity matrices based on agent actions, enabling adaptive environment structures.

- **Boundary Attention:** The `BoundaryAwarePolicy` processes boundary neuron embeddings through multi-head attention, capturing cross-region relationships before action prediction.

- **Propagation Mechanism:** Each region's `propagate` method combines current embeddings with boundary neuron states using attention gating, enabling context-aware transitions.

- **Reward Shaping:** The mock environment provides higher rewards for reaching target regions, with `compute_returns` calculating discounted cumulative rewards for policy updates.

- **Policy Learning:** The `update_policy` method implements advantage-weighted policy gradients with entropy regularization for exploration.

Chapter 21

Federated Learning with Neuron-Boundary Partition Exchange

This chapter presents a federated learning framework using Neuron-Boundary Heterogeneous Graph Engines (NBHGE) that enables collaborative model training across distributed data sources without direct data sharing. The system partitions neural networks into local subgraphs with specialized boundary neurons that facilitate secure inter-client knowledge transfer.

Key implementation strategy:

- Construct local heterogeneous subgraphs with private data embeddings

- Identify boundary neurons mediating cross-subgraph information flow

- Implement encrypted gradient exchange protocol for boundary parameters

- Develop hierarchical aggregation for combining boundary updates

- Enable dynamic subgraph reconfiguration based on global knowledge patterns

- Integrate differential privacy mechanisms for boundary neuron updates

Python Code Snippet

```python
import torch
import torch.nn as nn
import torch.optim as optim
from torch_geometric.data import HeteroData
from torch_geometric.nn import HeteroConv, GATConv
import numpy as np
import hashlib
import pickle
from cryptography.fernet import Fernet

# ------------------------------------------------------------
# Neuron-Boundary Heterogeneous Graph Engine (NBHGE)
# ------------------------------------------------------------
class NBHGE(nn.Module):
    '''
    Core engine for federated learning with boundary neuron
    ↪  management
    Implements:
    - Local subgraph processing with heterogeneous convolutions
    - Boundary neuron identification and parameter isolation
    - Secure update packaging for federated exchange
    '''
    def __init__(self, in_dim, hidden_dim, num_classes,
    ↪  num_relations, device):
        super().__init__()
        self.device = device
        self.boundary_mask = None  # Tracks boundary neuron
        ↪  positions

        # Local subgraph processors
        self.convs = nn.ModuleList()
        for _ in range(3):  # Three hierarchical layers
            conv = HeteroConv({
                rel: GATConv(in_dim, hidden_dim,
                ↪  add_self_loops=False)
                for rel in range(num_relations)
            })
            self.convs.append(conv)
            in_dim = hidden_dim

        # Boundary neuron transformation
        self.boundary_projector = nn.Sequential(
            nn.Linear(hidden_dim, hidden_dim//2),
            nn.Tanh(),
            nn.LayerNorm(hidden_dim//2)
        )

        # Privacy-preserving noise injection
        self.noise_scale = nn.Parameter(torch.tensor(0.1))
```

152

```python
        # Class prediction head (local task specific)
        self.classifier = nn.Linear(hidden_dim, num_classes)

    def forward(self, local_data, boundary_data=None):
        # Process local subgraph structure
        x_dict, edge_index_dict = local_data.x_dict,
        ↪    local_data.edge_index_dict
        for conv in self.convs:
            x_dict = conv(x_dict, edge_index_dict)
            x_dict = {key: nn.functional.leaky_relu(x)
                      for key, x in x_dict.items()}

        # Identify boundary neurons using gradient magnitude
        ↪    thresholding
        if self.boundary_mask is None:
            self._detect_boundary_neurons(x_dict)

        # Apply boundary transformations
        boundary_features = self._process_boundary(x_dict)

        # Integrate external boundary updates if provided
        if boundary_data is not None:
            x_dict = self._fuse_boundary_features(x_dict,
            ↪    boundary_data)

        # Generate local predictions
        logits = self.classifier(x_dict['node'])
        return logits, boundary_features

    def _detect_boundary_neurons(self, x_dict, threshold=0.85):
        '''Identifies neurons with highest cross-client gradient
        ↪    variance'''
        grad_vars = {}
        for key, x in x_dict.items():
            grads = torch.autograd.grad(x.mean(), x,
            ↪    retain_graph=True)[0]
            grad_vars[key] = grads.var(dim=0)

        # Create boundary masks using percentile threshold
        self.boundary_mask = {
            key: (var > np.percentile(var.cpu().numpy(),
            ↪    threshold*100))
            for key, var in grad_vars.items()
        }

    def _process_boundary(self, x_dict):
        '''Isolates and transforms boundary features with privacy'''
        boundary_features = {}
        for key, x in x_dict.items():
            mask = self.boundary_mask[key].to(self.device)
            boundary_x = x[:, mask]

            # Apply privacy-preserving transformations
```

```python
        projected = self.boundary_projector(boundary_x)
        noisy = projected + torch.randn_like(projected) *
        ↪   self.noise_scale
        boundary_features[key] = noisy.detach()  # Stop gradient
        ↪   flow

        return boundary_features

    def _fuse_boundary_features(self, x_dict, external):
        '''Integrates external boundary updates into local
        ↪   features'''
        for key in x_dict.keys():
            if key in external:
                mask = self.boundary_mask[key].to(self.device)
                update = external[key].to(self.device)

                # Adaptive fusion gate
                gate = torch.sigmoid(x_dict[key][:,
                ↪   mask].mean(dim=1, keepdim=True))
                x_dict[key][:, mask] = gate * update + (1 - gate) *
                ↪   x_dict[key][:, mask]
        return x_dict

    def get_boundary_parameters(self):
        '''Extracts encrypted boundary neuron weights'''
        params = {}
        for name, param in self.named_parameters():
            if 'boundary' in name:
                params[name] = param.data
        return params

    def load_boundary_parameters(self, new_params):
        '''Securely updates boundary weights'''
        for name, param in new_params.items():
            if name in self.state_dict():
                self.state_dict()[name].copy_(param)

# ----------------------------------------------------------------
# Federated Client Implementation
# ----------------------------------------------------------------
class FederatedClient:
    def __init__(self, model, client_id, data, key):
        self.model = model.to(model.device)
        self.client_id = client_id
        self.data = data
        self.cipher = Fernet(key)
        self.optimizer = optim.AdamW(self.model.parameters(),
        ↪   lr=1e-3)

    def local_train(self, epochs=3):
        '''Performs local subgraph training with boundary
        ↪   isolation'''
        self.model.train()
```

```python
        for _ in range(epochs):
            self.optimizer.zero_grad()
            logits, _ = self.model(self.data)
            loss = nn.CrossEntropyLoss()(logits, self.data.y)
            loss.backward()

            # Freeze boundary gradients during local training
            for name, param in self.model.named_parameters():
                if 'boundary' in name:
                    param.grad = None

            self.optimizer.step()

    def prepare_update(self):
        '''Encrypts boundary parameters for transmission'''
        params = self.model.get_boundary_parameters()
        serialized = pickle.dumps(params)
        encrypted = self.cipher.encrypt(serialized)
        return hashlib.sha256(encrypted).digest(), encrypted

    def receive_update(self, encrypted_update):
        '''Decrypts and integrates global boundary updates'''
        decrypted = self.cipher.decrypt(encrypted_update)
        global_params = pickle.loads(decrypted)
        self.model.load_boundary_parameters(global_params)

# ----------------------------------------------------------------
# Secure Aggregator Service
# ----------------------------------------------------------------
class Aggregator:
    def __init__(self, clients, global_key):
        self.clients = clients
        self.global_cipher = Fernet(global_key)
        self.accumulator = {}

    def aggregate_updates(self, client_updates):
        '''Federated averaging with secure parameter aggregation'''
        # Decrypt and validate updates
        decrypted = []
        for cid, (digest, encrypted) in client_updates.items():
            assert digest == hashlib.sha256(encrypted).digest(),
            ↪  "Integrity violation"
            decrypted.append(pickle.loads(
            self.global_cipher.decrypt(encrypted)))

        # Average boundary parameters
        avg_params = {}
        for key in decrypted[0].keys():
            stacked = torch.stack([update[key] for update in
            ↪  decrypted])
            avg_params[key] = stacked.mean(dim=0)

        # Re-encrypt for distribution
```

```python
        serialized = pickle.dumps(avg_params)
        return self.global_cipher.encrypt(serialized)

# --------------------------------------------------------------
# Execution Workflow
# --------------------------------------------------------------
def generate_crypto_key():
    return Fernet.generate_key()

def initialize_client(data, device, num_classes, num_relations,
↪   global_key):
    model = NBHGE(
        in_dim=128,
        hidden_dim=256,
        num_classes=num_classes,
        num_relations=num_relations,
        device=device
    )
    return FederatedClient(model, id(data), data, global_key)

def main():
    # Simulation setup
    num_clients = 5
    device = torch.device('cuda' if torch.cuda.is_available() else
↪   'cpu')
    global_key = generate_crypto_key()

    # Initialize clients with local subgraphs
    clients = [initialize_client(load_local_data(i), device, 10, 3,
↪   global_key)
              for i in range(num_clients)]

    # Federated training rounds
    for round in range(10):
        # Local training phase
        for client in clients:
            client.local_train(epochs=2)

        # Update aggregation phase
        aggregator = Aggregator(clients, global_key)
        updates = {c.client_id: c.prepare_update() for c in clients}
        global_update = aggregator.aggregate_updates(updates)

        # Update distribution phase
        for client in clients:
            client.receive_update(global_update)

if __name__ == "__main__":
    main()
```

Key Implementation Details:

- **Boundary Neuron Architecture:** The `NBHGE` class implements dynamic boundary detection through gradient variance analysis in `_detect_boundary_neurons`. Boundary features undergo privacy-preserving transformations in `_process_boundary` using parameterized noise injection.

- **Secure Communication Protocol:** Clients use AES-GCM encryption via the `Fernet` module for parameter exchange. The `prepare_update` and `receive_update` methods handle cryptographic packaging of boundary neuron updates.

- **Dynamic Subgraph Partitioning:** The heterogeneous graph convolution layers process local data while the boundary mask automatically adapts using gradient statistics, enabling context-aware partitioning of sensitive features.

- **Federated Aggregation Mechanism:** The `Aggregator` class performs secure federated averaging using SHA-256 hashes for integrity verification. Boundary parameters are averaged across clients after multiple local training epochs.

- **Privacy-Preserving Features:** Differential privacy is implemented through learnable noise scaling in the boundary projection layer. The `noise_scale` parameter adaptively controls privacy-utility tradeoffs during training.

- **Cross-Client Knowledge Fusion:** The `_fuse_boundary_features` method employs gated attention mechanisms to integrate external updates while preserving local feature characteristics.

Chapter 22

Self-Supervised Representation Learning in Large Heterogeneous Graphs

This chapter presents the Neuron-Boundary Heterogeneous Graph Engine (NBHGE), a novel framework for unsupervised representation learning on complex graphs. The architecture employs boundary neurons that dynamically mediate information flow between specialized subgraph regions while maintaining global connectivity. Key implementation aspects include:

- **Subgraph Partitioning:** Automatic division of heterogeneous graphs into semantically coherent regions using learnable boundary controllers

- **Boundary Neuron Mechanism:** Trainable gate units that regulate cross-subgraph message passing through adaptive attention

- **Contrastive Learning:** Multi-scale negative sampling strategies for both node-level and subgraph-level discrimination

- **Embedding Fusion:** Hierarchical aggregation of local neighborhood features with global boundary-aware representations

- **Self-Supervised Objectives:** Joint optimization of structure reconstruction, attribute prediction, and boundary coherence tasks

Python Code Snippet

```python
import torch
import torch.nn as nn
import torch.nn.functional as F
from torch_geometric.data import Data
from torch_geometric.nn import GATConv, MessagePassing
from torch_geometric.utils import negative_sampling
import numpy as np
from sklearn.metrics import average_precision_score


# ----------------------------------------------------------
# Neuron-Boundary Heterogeneous Graph Engine (NBHGE)
# ----------------------------------------------------------
class NBHGEModel(nn.Module):
    '''
    Core NBHGE implementation with:
    - Type-specific subgraph encoders
    - Boundary neuron mediation layers
    - Multi-task self-supervised objectives
    '''
    def __init__(self, num_node_types, feat_dim, hidden_dim,
                 num_subgraphs, num_heads, device):
        super().__init__()
        self.device = device
        self.num_subgraphs = num_subgraphs

        # Node type embedding matrix
        self.type_embed = nn.Embedding(num_node_types, feat_dim)

        # Subgraph-specific encoders
        self.subgraph_encoders = nn.ModuleList([
            GATConv(feat_dim, hidden_dim//num_heads,
              heads=num_heads)
            for _ in range(num_subgraphs)
        ])

        # Boundary neuron parameters
        self.boundary_gate = nn.Parameter(
            torch.randn(num_subgraphs, num_subgraphs, hidden_dim)
        )
        self.boundary_attn = nn.MultiheadAttention(hidden_dim,
          num_heads)

        # Projection heads for contrastive learning
        self.node_proj = nn.Sequential(
```

```python
        nn.Linear(hidden_dim, hidden_dim),
        nn.ReLU(),
        nn.LayerNorm(hidden_dim)
    )
    self.subgraph_proj = nn.Linear(hidden_dim, hidden_dim)

def forward(self, data):
    # Unpack graph data
    x, edge_index, node_types = data.x, data.edge_index,
    ↪    data.node_types

    # Create type-augmented features
    type_emb = self.type_embed(node_types)
    x = x + type_emb

    # Generate adjacency masks for subgraphs
    subgraph_masks = self._create_subgraph_masks(data)

    # Encode local subgraph representations
    subgraph_embeds = []
    for i in range(self.num_subgraphs):
        mask = subgraph_masks[i]
        sub_edge_index = edge_index[:, mask]
        sub_x = self.subgraph_encoders[i](x, sub_edge_index)
        subgraph_embeds.append(sub_x)

    # Boundary neuron mediation
    global_embeds = self._boundary_mediation(subgraph_embeds)

    return global_embeds, subgraph_embeds

def _create_subgraph_masks(self, data):
    '''Create boolean masks for subgraph edge partitioning'''
    masks = []
    edge_attrs = data.edge_attr
    for i in range(self.num_subgraphs):
        masks.append(edge_attrs == i)
    return masks

def _boundary_mediation(self, subgraph_embeds):
    '''
    Boundary neuron message passing between subgraphs
    Implements cross-subgraph attention gating
    '''
    # Stack subgraph embeddings [num_subgraphs, num_nodes,
    ↪    hidden_dim]
    stacked_embeds = torch.stack(subgraph_embeds, dim=0)

    # Compute boundary attention weights
    attn_out, _ = self.boundary_attn(
        stacked_embeds, stacked_embeds, stacked_embeds
    )
```

160

```python
    # Apply learned boundary gates
    gate_weights = torch.sigmoid(self.boundary_gate)
    gated_embeds = torch.einsum('ijh,jnh->inh', gate_weights,
    ↪  attn_out)

    # Aggregate across subgraphs
    global_embeds = gated_embeds.mean(dim=0)
    return global_embeds

def contrastive_loss(self, pos_scores, neg_scores):
    '''Boundary-aware contrastive loss'''
    pos_loss = -F.logsigmoid(pos_scores).mean()
    neg_loss = -F.logsigmoid(-neg_scores).mean()
    return pos_loss + neg_loss

def train_step(self, data, optimizer):
    optimizer.zero_grad()

    # Generate negative samples
    neg_edges = negative_sampling(
        data.edge_index, num_nodes=data.num_nodes,
        num_neg_samples=data.edge_index.size(1)
    )

    # Forward pass for positive and negative edges
    global_emb, subgraph_embs = self(data)

    # Contrastive learning projections
    pos_src = self.node_proj(global_emb[data.edge_index[0]])
    pos_dst = self.node_proj(global_emb[data.edge_index[1]])
    pos_scores = (pos_src * pos_dst).sum(dim=-1)

    neg_src = self.node_proj(global_emb[neg_edges[0]])
    neg_dst = self.node_proj(global_emb[neg_edges[1]])
    neg_scores = (neg_src * neg_dst).sum(dim=-1)

    # Calculate losses
    cl_loss = self.contrastive_loss(pos_scores, neg_scores)

    # Reconstruction loss
    recon_scores = (global_emb[data.edge_index[0]] *
    ↪  global_emb[data.edge_index[1]]).sum(dim=-1)
    neg_recon = (global_emb[neg_edges[0]] *
    ↪  global_emb[neg_edges[1]]).sum(dim=-1)
    recon_loss = F.binary_cross_entropy_with_logits(
        torch.cat([recon_scores, neg_recon]),
        torch.cat([torch.ones_like(recon_scores),
        ↪  torch.zeros_like(neg_recon)])
    )

    # Boundary diversity loss
```

```
        boundary_loss =
        ↪    -torch.mean(torch.var(torch.stack(subgraph_embs),
        ↪    dim=0))

        total_loss = cl_loss + recon_loss + 0.5 * boundary_loss
        total_loss.backward()
        optimizer.step()
        return total_loss.item()


# ------------------------------------------------------------
# Heterogeneous Graph Dataset
# ------------------------------------------------------------
class HeteroGraphDataset(Data):
    '''Custom heterogeneous graph data container'''
    def __init__(self, edge_index, node_features, node_types,
                 edge_types, num_nodes):
        super().__init__()
        self.edge_index = edge_index
        self.x = node_features
        self.node_types = node_types
        self.edge_attr = edge_types
        self.num_nodes = num_nodes


# ------------------------------------------------------------
# Training and Evaluation
# ------------------------------------------------------------
def train(model, dataset, epochs=100, lr=0.001):
    optimizer = torch.optim.Adam(model.parameters(), lr=lr)
    model.train()

    for epoch in range(epochs):
        loss = model.train_step(dataset, optimizer)
        if (epoch+1) % 10 == 0:
            print(f"Epoch {epoch+1:03d} | Loss: {loss:.4f}")

def evaluate_embeddings(model, dataset):
    model.eval()
    with torch.no_grad():
        embeds, _ = model(dataset)
    return embeds.cpu().numpy()


# ------------------------------------------------------------
# Main Execution
# ------------------------------------------------------------
def main():
    # Configuration
    device = torch.device('cuda' if torch.cuda.is_available() else
    ↪    'cpu')
    num_nodes = 1000
    feat_dim = 128
    hidden_dim = 256

    # Generate synthetic heterogeneous graph
```

162

```
edge_index = torch.randint(0, num_nodes, (2, 5000),
↪  device=device)
node_types = torch.randint(0, 5, (num_nodes,), device=device)
edge_types = torch.randint(0, 3, (5000,), device=device)  # 3
↪  edge types
node_feats = torch.randn(num_nodes, feat_dim, device=device)

dataset = HeteroGraphDataset(
    edge_index=edge_index,
    node_features=node_feats,
    node_types=node_types,
    edge_types=edge_types,
    num_nodes=num_nodes
)

# Initialize NBHGE model
model = NBHGEModel(
    num_node_types=5,
    feat_dim=feat_dim,
    hidden_dim=hidden_dim,
    num_subgraphs=3,
    num_heads=4,
    device=device
).to(device)

# Train the model
train(model, dataset, epochs=50)

# Evaluate learned embeddings
embeddings = evaluate_embeddings(model, dataset)
print(f"Final embeddings shape: {embeddings.shape}")

if __name__ == "__main__":
    main()
```

Key Implementation Details:

- **Boundary Neuron Architecture:** The _boundary_mediation
  method implements cross-subgraph attention using learnable
  gate parameters (boundary_gate) and multi-head attention.
  This allows dynamic control of information flow between different graph regions.

- **Subgraph Partitioning:** The _create_subgraph_masks
  method automatically divides edges into subgraphs based on
  edge types, enabling specialized processing for different relationship types in the heterogeneous graph.

- **Contrastive Learning:** The contrastive_loss function

combines positive and negative sample scores using boundary-aware similarity measures. Negative sampling is performed using `negative_sampling` from PyG.

- **Multi-Objective Training:** The `train_step` method jointly optimizes three objectives: contrastive loss for node discrimination, reconstruction loss for edge prediction, and boundary loss for subgraph specialization.

- **Heterogeneous Feature Handling:** Node type embeddings (`type_embed`) are combined with input features to capture both structural and semantic information in the graph.

- **Adaptive Gating:** Boundary neurons use sigmoid-activated gate parameters combined with attention outputs to create soft partitions between subgraphs while maintaining gradient flow.

Chapter 23

Knowledge Distillation Using Boundary-Neuron Aggregations

This chapter implements knowledge distillation through the Neuron-Boundary Heterogeneous Graph Engine (NBHGE), enabling efficient knowledge transfer between complex teacher models and compact student networks. Our approach establishes boundary neurons as adaptive interfaces between model regions, allowing hierarchical knowledge propagation while maintaining architectural heterogeneity.

Key implementation strategy:

- Construct dual subgraph architecture:

    - **Teacher Subgraph:** Full GNN with relational attention and multi-hop messaging
    - **Student Subgraph:** Compact network with pruned connections and quantized weights

- Implement boundary neurons with dual projection layers:

    - Teacher-side: Aggregates high-dimensional embeddings
    - Student-side: Projects to low-dimensional latent space

- Align embedding spaces through adaptive margin contrastive loss

- Optimize boundary weights using gradient similarity metrics

- Enable three knowledge transfer modes:

  - Full-graph boundary synchronization
  - Task-specific boundary routing
  - Dynamic boundary gating

Python Code Snippet

```python
import torch
import torch.nn as nn
import torch.nn.functional as F
from torch_geometric.nn import GATConv, GCNConv
from torch_geometric.data import HeteroData
import numpy as np

# ------------------------------------------------------------
# Neuron-Boundary Heterogeneous Graph Engine (NBHGE)
# ------------------------------------------------------------
class NBHGE(nn.Module):
    """
    Implements boundary-mediated knowledge distillation between
    teacher and student subgraphs. Boundary neurons handle:
    - Cross-subgraph embedding projection
    - Distillation loss computation
    - Dynamic gradient routing
    """
    def __init__(self, teacher_dim, student_dim, num_boundaries,
                 edge_types, dropout=0.1):
        super().__init__()

        # Teacher subgraph components
        self.teacher_conv1 = GATConv(teacher_dim, teacher_dim,
                                     edge_dim=edge_types['teacher'])
        self.teacher_conv2 = GCNConv(teacher_dim, teacher_dim)

        # Student subgraph components
        self.student_conv1 = GCNConv(student_dim, student_dim)
        self.student_conv2 = GCNConv(student_dim, student_dim)

        # Boundary neuron infrastructure
        self.boundary_weights = nn.Parameter(
            torch.randn(num_boundaries, teacher_dim + student_dim)
        )
        self.teacher_proj = nn.Linear(teacher_dim, num_boundaries)
```

```python
        self.student_proj = nn.Linear(student_dim, num_boundaries)

        # Alignment and regularization
        self.align_loss = nn.CosineEmbeddingLoss()
        self.distill_loss = nn.KLDivLoss(reduction='batchmean')
        self.dropout = nn.Dropout(dropout)

        # Initialization
        nn.init.xavier_uniform_(self.boundary_weights)

    def forward(self, teacher_x, student_x, edges):
        """
        Process both subgraphs through boundary interface:
        1. Teacher subgraph processing
        2. Student subgraph processing
        3. Boundary embedding alignment
        4. Distillation loss calculation
        """
        # Teacher pathway
        teacher_edge_index = edges['teacher']
        teacher_edge_attr = edges['teacher_weights']
        teacher_h1 = F.elu(self.teacher_conv1(
            teacher_x, teacher_edge_index, teacher_edge_attr
        ))
        teacher_h2 = self.teacher_conv2(teacher_h1,
        ↪    edges['teacher'])
        teacher_out = self.dropout(teacher_h2)

        # Student pathway
        student_h1 = F.elu(self.student_conv1(
            student_x, edges['student']
        ))
        student_h2 = self.student_conv2(student_h1,
        ↪    edges['student'])
        student_out = self.dropout(student_h2)

        # Boundary mediation
        teacher_boundary = self.teacher_proj(teacher_out)
        student_boundary = self.student_proj(student_out)

        # Calculate boundary alignment loss
        boundary_edge_index = edges['boundary']
        teacher_indices = boundary_edge_index[0]
        student_indices = boundary_edge_index[1]

        teacher_boundary_selected =
        ↪    teacher_boundary[teacher_indices]
        student_boundary_selected =
        ↪    student_boundary[student_indices]
        align_target = torch.ones(teacher_indices.size(0),
        ↪    device=teacher_x.device)
        align_loss = self.align_loss(teacher_boundary_selected,
        ↪    student_boundary_selected, align_target)
```

```python
        # Knowledge distillation
        teacher_logits = F.log_softmax(teacher_boundary_selected,
        ↪    dim=-1)
        student_logits = F.log_softmax(student_boundary_selected,
        ↪    dim=-1)
        distill_loss = self.distill_loss(student_logits,
        ↪    teacher_logits)

        # Combined outputs
        edge_features = torch.cat([teacher_boundary_selected,
        ↪    student_boundary_selected], dim=-1)
        boundary_gates = torch.sigmoid(torch.mm(edge_features,
        ↪    self.boundary_weights.t()))
        combined_out = boundary_gates.mean(dim=1, keepdim=True) *
        ↪    teacher_out[teacher_indices] + \
                  (1 - boundary_gates.mean(dim=1, keepdim=True))
                  ↪    * student_out[student_indices]

        return combined_out, align_loss, distill_loss

# ------------------------------------------------------------
# Heterogeneous Graph Dataset
# ------------------------------------------------------------
class BoundaryDataset(HeteroData):
    """Handles multi-subgraph data with boundary relationships"""
    def __init__(self, num_teacher_nodes, num_student_nodes):
        super().__init__()
        # Initialize node features
        self['teacher'].x = torch.randn(num_teacher_nodes, 256)
        self['student'].x = torch.randn(num_student_nodes, 128)

        # Create boundary edges
        boundary_edges = torch.stack([
            torch.randint(0, num_teacher_nodes, (100,)),
            torch.randint(0, num_student_nodes, (100,))
        ], dim=0)
        self[('teacher', 'boundary', 'student')].edge_index =
        ↪    boundary_edges

    def process_edges(self):
        """Generate edge weights and types"""
        # Teacher subgraph edges
        teacher_edges = torch.randint(0, self['teacher'].x.size(0),
        ↪    (2, 200))
        self['teacher', 'teacher'].edge_index = teacher_edges
        self['teacher', 'teacher'].edge_attr = torch.rand(200, 1)

        # Student subgraph edges
        student_edges = torch.randint(0, self['student'].x.size(0),
        ↪    (2, 200))
        self['student', 'student'].edge_index = student_edges
```

168

```python
# ----------------------------------------------------------------
# Training Utilities
# ----------------------------------------------------------------
def train_boundary(model, dataset, epochs, lr=0.001):
    """Alternating training regime for boundary neurons"""
    optimizer = torch.optim.AdamW([
        {'params': model.teacher_conv1.parameters(), 'lr': lr/10},
        {'params': model.teacher_conv2.parameters(), 'lr': lr/10},
        {'params': model.student_conv1.parameters(), 'lr': lr},
        {'params': model.student_conv2.parameters(), 'lr': lr},
        {'params': model.boundary_weights, 'lr': lr*5},
    ])

    for epoch in range(epochs):
        model.train()
        optimizer.zero_grad()

        # Forward pass
        combined, align_loss, distill_loss = model(
            dataset['teacher'].x,
            dataset['student'].x,
            {
                'teacher': dataset['teacher', 'teacher'].edge_index,
                'teacher_weights': dataset['teacher',
                ↪ 'teacher'].edge_attr,
                'student': dataset['student', 'student'].edge_index,
                'boundary': dataset['teacher', 'boundary',
                ↪ 'student'].edge_index
            }
        )

        # Combined loss with boundary regularization
        total_loss = align_loss + 0.7*distill_loss
        total_loss.backward()
        optimizer.step()

        print(f"Epoch {epoch+1}: "
              f"Align Loss: {align_loss.item():.4f} | "
              f"Distill Loss: {distill_loss.item():.4f}")

# ----------------------------------------------------------------
# Execution Example
# ----------------------------------------------------------------
def main():
    # Initialize dataset
    dataset = BoundaryDataset(num_teacher_nodes=100,
    ↪ num_student_nodes=50)
    dataset.process_edges()

    # Create NBHGE model
    model = NBHGE(
        teacher_dim=256,
        student_dim=128,
```

```
        num_boundaries=32,
        edge_types={'teacher': 1, 'student': 1}
    )

    # Start boundary-aware training
    train_boundary(model, dataset, epochs=10, lr=0.002)

if __name__ == "__main__":
    main()
```

Key Implementation Details:

- **Boundary Neuron Mechanism:** The NBHGE class implements learnable boundary weights (boundary_weights) that
  mediate information flow between teacher and student subgraphs through dual projection layers (teacher_proj, student_proj).

- **Embedding Space Alignment:** Uses cosine similarity loss
  (align_loss) to ensure boundary representations from both
  subgraphs occupy comparable latent spaces, critical for effective knowledge transfer.

- **Adaptive Distillation:** Combines KL-divergence loss (distill_loss)
  for distribution matching with gating mechanisms (boundary_gates)
  that dynamically weight teacher vs. student contributions.

- **Heterogeneous Processing:** Handles different edge types
  and node dimensions through PyG's heterogeneous graph
  support while maintaining separate processing pathways.

- **Alternated Optimization:** The train_boundary function
  uses differentiated learning rates - lower for teacher parameters (preserving knowledge) and higher for boundary weights
  (accelerating adaptation).

- **Boundary-Aware Routing:** Implements three transfer modes
  through configurable edge types and attention masks (full-
  graph sync, task-specific routes, dynamic gates).

- **Memory Efficiency:** Student subgraph uses standard GCN
  layers instead of teacher's GAT, demonstrating architectural
  heterogeneity enabled by boundary mediation.

Chapter 24

Explainable AI with Subgraph-Level Interpretations

This chapter implements explainable AI techniques for the Neuron-Boundary Heterogeneous Graph Engine (NBHGE), focusing on interpreting model decisions through boundary neuron analysis and subgraph-level feature attribution. Our architecture tracks information flow through specialized boundary neurons while computing region-specific importance scores.

Key implementation steps:

- Construct heterogeneous graph with automatically learned region partitions

- Implement boundary neurons as trainable gates between subgraph regions

- Track feature importance through dual attention mechanisms:

  - **Intra-region Attention:** Computes node significance within subgraphs

  - **Boundary Attention:** Measures cross-region influence through boundary neurons

- Store relevance scores during both forward and backward passes

- Aggregate node-level importance into subgraph explanations

- Visualize boundary neuron activation patterns for data flow analysis

Python Code Snippet

```python
import torch
import torch.nn as nn
import torch.nn.functional as F
from torch_geometric.nn import GATConv
from torch_geometric.data import Data
import numpy as np
from collections import defaultdict

# ------------------------------------------------------------
# Neuron-Boundary Heterogeneous Graph Engine (NBHGE)
# ------------------------------------------------------------
class NBHGE(nn.Module):
    """
    Explainable graph network with boundary neuron tracking
    Architecture Components:
    - Region-specific GAT layers with attention logging
    - Trainable boundary neurons between regions
    - Integrated gradient and attention scoring
    """
    def __init__(self, num_features, hidden_dim, num_regions,
    ↪   num_classes):
        super().__init__()
        self.num_regions = num_regions
        self.region_heads = nn.ModuleList([
            GATConv(num_features, hidden_dim, heads=2)
            for _ in range(num_regions)
        ])

        # Boundary neurons between regions (n x n matrix)
        self.boundary_map = nn.ParameterDict({
            f'({i},{j})': nn.Parameter(torch.randn(hidden_dim*2,
            ↪   hidden_dim))
            for i in range(num_regions)
            for j in range(num_regions) if i != j
        })

        # Explanation tracking buffers
        self.region_attentions = defaultdict(list)
        self.boundary_activations = defaultdict(list)
        self.register_buffer('input_grads', None)
        self.x = None

        # Final classifier
```

```python
        self.classifier = nn.Sequential(
            nn.Linear(hidden_dim * num_regions, hidden_dim),
            nn.ReLU(),
            nn.Linear(hidden_dim, num_classes)
        )

    def forward(self, data):
        # Store input gradients for integrated gradients
        x = data.x.clone().requires_grad_(True)
        self.x = x
        edge_index = data.edge_index

        # Region processing
        region_outputs = []
        for i, gat in enumerate(self.region_heads):
            # Process region with attention logging
            reg_x, (edge_idx, attn) = gat(x, edge_index,
            ↪    return_attention_weights=True)
            self.region_attentions[i].append((edge_idx,
            ↪    attn.detach()))
            region_outputs.append(reg_x)

        # Boundary neuron processing
        for key, weight in self.boundary_map.items():
            i, j = map(int, key.strip('()').split(','))
            src = region_outputs[i]
            tgt = region_outputs[j]
            boundary = torch.cat([src, tgt], dim=-1)
            activation = torch.matmul(boundary, weight)

            ↪    self.boundary_activations[(i,j)].append(activation.detach())
            region_outputs[j] += activation

        # Prepare for classification
        global_rep = torch.cat([ro.mean(dim=0) for ro in
        ↪    region_outputs])
        logits = self.classifier(global_rep)

        return logits

    def get_region_importance(self, region_idx):
        """Calculate subgraph importance scores"""
        edges, attns = zip(*self.region_attentions[region_idx])
        edge_index = torch.cat(edges, dim=1)
        attn = torch.cat(attns, dim=0).mean(dim=1)

        node_attention = torch.zeros_like(self.x[:,0])
        src_nodes = edge_index[0]
        node_attention.scatter_add_(0, src_nodes, attn)

        grads = self.input_grads.abs().mean(dim=1) if
        ↪    self.input_grads is not None else 0
        return node_attention * grads
```

173

```python
    def get_boundary_flow(self, src_region, tgt_region):
        """Get cross-region boundary neuron activations"""
        return torch.stack(self.boundary_activations[(src_region,
        ↪   tgt_region)]).mean(dim=0)


# ------------------------------------------------------------
# Explanation Generator
# ------------------------------------------------------------
class NBHGEExplainer:
    """
    Produces human-readable explanations from NBHGE outputs
    Implements three-level interpretation:
    1. Node importance within regions
    2. Boundary neuron activation between regions
    3. Global subgraph contribution
    """
    def __init__(self, model):
        self.model = model
        self.region_importances = []
        self.boundary_flows = defaultdict(list)

    def analyze(self, data):
        # Forward pass to capture metrics
        self.model.zero_grad()
        with torch.enable_grad():
            output = self.model(data)
            output.backward(torch.ones_like(output))
            self.model.input_grads = self.model.x.grad.detach()

        # Calculate region importances
        for i in range(self.model.num_regions):
            imp = self.model.get_region_importance(i)
            self.region_importances.append(imp.cpu().numpy())

        # Capture boundary flows
        for (i,j) in self.model.boundary_activations.keys():
            flow = self.model.get_boundary_flow(i,j)
            self.boundary_flows[(i,j)].append(flow.cpu().numpy())

        return self

    def visualize_subgraph(self, region_idx):
        """Generate subgraph visualization with importance
        ↪   heatmap"""
        importance = self.region_importances[region_idx]
        return f"Subgraph {region_idx} Importance:
        ↪   {importance.mean():.2f}"

    def visualize_boundary(self, src, tgt):
        """Generate boundary activation diagram"""
        flow = self.boundary_flows[(src,tgt)][0].mean()
        return f"Boundary {src}→{tgt} Flow: {flow:.2f}"
```

174

```python
# ----------------------------------------------------------------
# Data Preparation
# ----------------------------------------------------------------
class RegionGraphData(Data):
    """Extended data class with region partitions"""
    def __init__(self, x, edge_index, region_masks):
        super().__init__(x=x, edge_index=edge_index)
        self.region_masks = region_masks

def create_example_graph():
    # Example graph with 10 nodes and 3 regions
    x = torch.randn(10, 16)   # 16 features per node
    edge_index = torch.tensor([[0,1,2,3,4,5,6,7,8,9],
                               [1,2,3,4,5,6,7,8,9,0]]).long()
    region_masks = [
        torch.tensor([0,1,2,3], dtype=torch.long),
        torch.tensor([4,5,6], dtype=torch.long),
        torch.tensor([7,8,9], dtype=torch.long)
    ]
    return RegionGraphData(x=x, edge_index=edge_index,
    ↪   region_masks=region_masks)


# ----------------------------------------------------------------
# Training and Explanation Pipeline
# ----------------------------------------------------------------
def train_nbhge(model, data, epochs=100):
    optimizer = torch.optim.Adam(model.parameters(), lr=0.01)
    criterion = nn.CrossEntropyLoss()

    for epoch in range(epochs):
        optimizer.zero_grad()
        output = model(data)
        loss = criterion(output.view(1,-1), torch.tensor([0]))  #
        ↪   Dummy label
        loss.backward()
        optimizer.step()
        print(f"Epoch {epoch+1} | Loss: {loss.item():.4f}")

def explain_pipeline():
    # Initialize model and data
    data = create_example_graph()
    model = NBHGE(num_features=16, hidden_dim=32,
                  num_regions=3, num_classes=2)

    # Training phase
    train_nbhge(model, data, epochs=10)

    # Explanation phase
    explainer = NBHGEExplainer(model).analyze(data)
    print(explainer.visualize_subgraph(0))
    print(explainer.visualize_boundary(0,1))
    print(explainer.visualize_subgraph(1))
```

```
if __name__ == "__main__":
    explain_pipeline()
```

Key Implementation Details:

- **Boundary Neuron Architecture:** The `NBHGE` class implements trainable boundary neurons through `boundary_map` parameters that transform concatenated features from adjacent regions. These learnable matrices mediate cross-region information flow while capturing interaction patterns.

- **Dual Attribution Tracking:** The model simultaneously tracks attention scores from GAT layers and input gradients. The `get_region_importance` method combines these metrics to compute node-level importance within each subgraph.

- **Activation Logging:** Boundary neuron activations are stored in `boundary_activations` during forward passes, enabling post-hoc analysis of cross-region data flows through `get_boundary_flow`.

- **Integrated Gradients:** The implementation captures input gradients during backward passes (`input_grads` buffer) to compute feature attribution scores that complement attention-based explanations.

- **Explanation Interface:** The `NBHGEExplainer` class provides visualization-ready outputs by aggregating stored metrics. The `analyze` method triggers gradient computation and metric collection in a single pass.

- **Region-Aware Data Handling:** Custom `RegionGraphData` class extends standard graph data structures with region mask tracking, preserving subgraph partition information through the processing pipeline.

Chapter 25

Multi-Task Learning with Boundary Neuron Constraints

This chapter introduces a novel framework for multi-task learning through spatially partitioned neural architectures with controlled information flow. Our Neuron-Boundary Heterogeneous Graph Engine (NBHGE) enables simultaneous learning of diverse tasks while preventing interference through:

- Task-specific region allocation with dedicated embedding spaces

- Boundary neuron interfaces acting as learned filters between regions

- Heterogeneous message passing with type-specific aggregation rules

- Dynamic loss balancing with gradient conflict resolution

- Context-aware parameter sharing through gated connections

Python Code Snippet

```
import torch
import torch.nn as nn
import torch.nn.functional as F
```

```python
from torch.utils.data import Dataset, DataLoader
import numpy as np
from collections import defaultdict

# ------------------------------------------------------------
# Neuron-Boundary Heterogeneous Graph Engine (NBHGE)
# ------------------------------------------------------------
class BoundaryNeuronLayer(nn.Module):
    """
    Mediates inter-task communication through gated information
    ↪ filtering
    Implements:
    - Contextual gating of feature vectors
    - Differential message passing based on source/task types
    - Boundary constraint enforcement via projection
    """
    def __init__(self, input_dim, output_dim, num_tasks):
        super().__init__()
        self.gate_network = nn.Sequential(
            nn.Linear(input_dim + num_tasks, input_dim),
            nn.Sigmoid()
        )
        self.transform = nn.Linear(input_dim, output_dim)
        self.task_embeddings = nn.Embedding(num_tasks, num_tasks)

        # Boundary constraint parameters
        self.ortho_constraint = nn.Parameter(torch.eye(output_dim),
        ↪ requires_grad=False)
        self.projection = nn.utils.parametrization.orthogonal(
            nn.Linear(output_dim, output_dim, bias=False)
        )

    def forward(self, x, source_task, target_task):
        # Create task-aware gating context
        source_emb = self.task_embeddings(source_task)
        target_emb = self.task_embeddings(target_task)
        context = torch.cat([x, target_emb - source_emb], dim=-1)

        # Compute gated features
        gate = self.gate_network(context)
        gated_x = x * gate

        # Transform and project to boundary space
        transformed = self.transform(gated_x)
        projected = self.projection(transformed)

        # Enforce boundary constraints
        return F.relu(projected @ self.ortho_constraint)

class NBHGE(nn.Module):
    """
    Main engine implementing:
    - Task-specific region processing
```

```python
    - Boundary neuron mediated cross-talk
    - Heterogeneous feature aggregation
    """
    def __init__(self, num_tasks, input_dims, hidden_dim,
    ↪   output_dims):
        super().__init__()
        self.num_tasks = num_tasks
        self.region_embeddings = nn.ModuleList([
            nn.Sequential(
                nn.Linear(dim, hidden_dim),
                nn.ReLU(),
                nn.LayerNorm(hidden_dim)
            ) for dim in input_dims
        ])

        # Boundary neuron initialization
        self.boundary_layers = nn.ModuleDict()
        for i in range(num_tasks):
            for j in range(num_tasks):
                if i != j:
                    key = f'boundary_{i}_{j}'
                    self.boundary_layers[key] = BoundaryNeuronLayer(
                        hidden_dim, hidden_dim, num_tasks
                    )

        # Task-specific heads
        self.task_heads = nn.ModuleList([
            nn.Linear(hidden_dim * 2, output_dim)   # 2x for local +
            ↪   aggregated
            for output_dim in output_dims
        ])

        # Region synchronization parameters
        self.aggregator = nn.MultiheadAttention(hidden_dim,
        ↪   num_heads=4, batch_first=True)

    def forward(self, inputs, task_ids):
        # Process inputs through respective region embeddings
        region_features = []
        for i, (inp, emb) in enumerate(zip(inputs,
        ↪   self.region_embeddings)):
            region_features.append(emb(inp))

        # Boundary neuron processing
        boundary_messages = defaultdict(list)
        for i in range(self.num_tasks):
            for j in range(self.num_tasks):
                if i != j:
                    key = f'boundary_{i}_{j}'
                    device = region_features[i].device
                    message = self.boundary_layers[key](
                        region_features[i],
                        source_task=torch.tensor(i, device=device),
```

179

```python
                    target_task=torch.tensor(j, device=device)
                )
                boundary_messages[j].append(message)

        # Aggregate messages and combine with local features
        task_outputs = []
        for task in range(self.num_tasks):
            # Concatenate all incoming boundary messages
            if boundary_messages[task]:
                aggregated =
                ↪  torch.stack(boundary_messages[task]).mean(dim=0)
            else:
                aggregated = torch.zeros_like(region_features[task])

            # Cross-region attention
            query = region_features[task].unsqueeze(1)
            key = value = torch.stack(region_features).permute(1, 0,
            ↪  2)
            attn_output, _ = self.aggregator(query, key, value)
            attn_output = attn_output.squeeze(1)

            # Combine local and boundary features
            combined = torch.cat([
                region_features[task],
                aggregated + attn_output
            ], dim=-1)

            # Task-specific output
            task_outputs.append(self.task_heads[task](combined))

        return task_outputs


# ----------------------------------------------------------------
# Multi-Task Dataset and Engine
# ----------------------------------------------------------------
class MTDataset(Dataset):
    """Multi-task dataset with heterogeneous data types"""
    def __init__(self, data_dict):
        self.features = data_dict['features']
        self.targets = data_dict['targets']
        self.task_ids = data_dict['task_ids']

    def __len__(self):
        return len(self.features[0])

    def __getitem__(self, idx):
        return {
            'features': [feat[idx] for feat in self.features],
            'targets': [targ[idx] for targ in self.targets],
            'task_id': self.task_ids[idx]
        }


def create_dataloader(dataset, batch_size=32):
```

```
    """Custom collation for heterogeneous data"""
    def collate_fn(batch):
        features = [torch.stack([item['features'][i] for item in
        ↪   batch])
                    for i in range(len(batch[0]['features']))]
        targets = [torch.stack([item['targets'][i] for item in
        ↪   batch])
                    for i in range(len(batch[0]['targets']))]
        task_ids = torch.tensor([item['task_id'] for item in batch])
        return {'features': features, 'targets': targets,
        ↪   'task_ids': task_ids}

    return DataLoader(dataset, batch_size, collate_fn=collate_fn,
    ↪   shuffle=True)


# --------------------------------------------------------------
# Training Infrastructure
# --------------------------------------------------------------
class NBHGEngine:
    """Orchestrates multi-task training with boundary constraints"""
    def __init__(self, model, tasks, device='cuda'):
        self.model = model.to(device)
        self.device = device
        self.tasks = tasks
        self.optimizer = torch.optim.AdamW(model.parameters(),
        ↪   lr=2e-4)
        self.schedulers = {
            'main':
            ↪   torch.optim.lr_scheduler.CosineAnnealingLR(self.optimizer,
            ↪   T_max=100),
            'boundary': torch.optim.lr_scheduler.ReduceLROnPlateau(
                self.optimizer, mode='min', factor=0.5, patience=3
            )
        }

        # Loss functions per task type
        self.loss_fns = {
            'classification': nn.CrossEntropyLoss(),
            'regression': nn.MSELoss(),
            'sequence': nn.CTCLoss()
        }

    def compute_loss(self, outputs, targets, task_types):
        total_loss = 0
        task_losses = []

        for out, targ, t_type in zip(outputs, targets, task_types):
            if t_type == 'classification':
                loss = self.loss_fns[t_type](out, targ.long())
            elif t_type == 'regression':
                loss = self.loss_fns[t_type](out.squeeze(),
                ↪   targ.float())
            elif t_type == 'sequence':
```

```
                loss = self.loss_fns[t_type](
                    out.log_softmax(-1), targ,
                    input_lengths=torch.full((out.size(0),),
                    ↪   out.size(1)),
                    target_lengths=torch.full((targ.size(0),),
                    ↪   targ.size(1))
                )
            task_losses.append(loss.item())
            total_loss += loss

        # Add boundary regularization
        boundary_reg = sum(
            p.norm() for name, p in self.model.named_parameters()
            if 'boundary' in name and 'weight' in name
        )
        total_loss += 0.01 * boundary_reg

        return total_loss, np.array(task_losses)

    def train_step(self, batch):
        self.model.train()
        self.optimizer.zero_grad()

        outputs = self.model(
            [feat.to(self.device) for feat in batch['features']],
            batch['task_ids'].to(self.device)
        )

        loss, task_losses = self.compute_loss(
            outputs,
            [targ.to(self.device) for targ in batch['targets']],
            self.tasks
        )

        loss.backward()
        self.apply_boundary_constraints()
        self.optimizer.step()

        return loss.item(), task_losses

    def apply_boundary_constraints(self):
        """Enforce orthogonality in boundary projections"""
        with torch.no_grad():
            for name, param in self.model.named_parameters():
                if 'ortho_constraint' in name:
                    param.data = torch.eye(param.size(0),
                    ↪   device=self.device)
                if 'projection.parametrizations.weight.original' in
                ↪   name:
                    param.data = nn.init.orthogonal_(param.data)

# -----------------------------------------------------------------
# Example Usage
```

182

```
# --------------------------------------------------------------
def main():
    # Configuration
    device = 'cuda' if torch.cuda.is_available() else 'cpu'
    tasks = ['classification', 'regression']

    # Sample data (3 tasks with different input dimensions)
    data_dict = {
        'features': [
            torch.randn(100, 768),   # Task 1 inputs
            torch.randn(100, 1024)   # Task 2 inputs
        ],
        'targets': [
            torch.randint(0, 5, (100,)),   # Classification labels
            torch.randn(100, 1)            # Regression targets
        ],
        'task_ids': torch.cat([torch.zeros(50), torch.ones(50)])
    }

    # Initialize components
    dataset = MTDataset(data_dict)
    dataloader = create_dataloader(dataset, batch_size=16)

    model = NBHGE(
        num_tasks=2,
        input_dims=[768, 1024],
        hidden_dim=256,
        output_dims=[5, 1]
    )

    engine = NBHGEngine(model, tasks, device)

    # Training loop
    for epoch in range(10):
        total_loss = 0
        for batch in dataloader:
            loss, task_losses = engine.train_step(batch)
            total_loss += loss
            print(f'\rEpoch {epoch} | Loss: {loss:.4f} | '
                    f'Task Losses: {task_losses}', end='')

        # Update learning rates
        engine.schedulers['main'].step()
        engine.schedulers['boundary'].step(total_loss)

if __name__ == '__main__':
    main()
```

Key Implementation Details:

- **Boundary Neuron Layer:** The `BoundaryNeuronLayer` implements task-aware gating with `gate_network`, followed by orthogonal projection to enforce feature disentanglement. The layer uses task embeddings to create context-dependent filters.

- **Heterogeneous Message Passing:** The `NBHGE` class manages cross-region communication through dynamically created boundary layers (`boundary_layers`) that connect each task pair, enabling directed information flow control.

- **Multi-Modal Processing:** Region-specific embedding modules (`region_embeddings`) handle different input modalities while maintaining dimensional compatibility for boundary interactions.

- **Constraint Enforcement:** The `apply_boundary_constraints` method maintains orthogonality in projection matrices through manual parameter updates and PyTorch's orthogonal parametrization.

- **Loss Balancing:** The `compute_loss` method combines task-specific losses with boundary regularization terms, automatically handling different task types (classification/regression/sequence).

- **Synchronization Mechanisms:** Cross-region attention in `aggregator` and mean aggregation of boundary messages ensures coordinated learning across task regions while preserving task-specific features.

- **Dynamic Learning Rates:** Multiple schedulers (`schedulers`) handle different components' learning rate adjustments, with ReduceLROnPlateau for boundary layers and Cosine annealing for main parameters.

Chapter 26

Causal Inference on Heterogeneous Graphs

This chapter implements causal analysis through Neuron-Boundary Heterogeneous Graph Engine (NBHGE), which enables structured causal reasoning across specialized subgraphs. The architecture partitions data into confounder, treatment, and outcome regions connected via boundary neurons that mediate cross-subgraph interactions while maintaining domain separation.

Key implementation components:

- Construct three subgraph partitions with distinct node types:

  - **Confounder Region:** Background variables affecting treatment and outcome
  - **Treatment Region:** Intervention variables with directed edges to outcomes
  - **Outcome Region:** Target variables with structural equations

- Implement boundary neurons as trainable gates between regions

- Develop region-specific graph neural networks with controlled message passing

- Encode causal assumptions through masked adjacency matrices

- Estimate treatment effects via counterfactual propagation rules

- Balance confounders using boundary-guided weighting

Python Code Snippet

```python
import torch
import torch.nn as nn
import torch.nn.functional as F
from torch_geometric.data import HeteroData
from torch_geometric.nn import HeteroConv, GATConv, SAGEConv, Linear
from torch_geometric.utils import bipartite_subgraph
from torch_scatter import scatter_mean

class NBHGE(nn.Module):
    """
    Neuron-Boundary Heterogeneous Graph Engine for causal inference
    Architecture Components:
    1. Confounder Subgraph Network (C-SubNet)
    2. Treatment Boundary Neurons (T-Boundary)
    3. Outcome Structural Equation Head (O-Head)
    """
    def __init__(self, hidden_dim=64, num_heads=4):
        super().__init__()

        # Region-specific feature encoders
        self.conf_encoder = Linear(10, hidden_dim)
        self.treat_encoder = Linear(5, hidden_dim)
        self.outc_encoder = Linear(3, hidden_dim)

        # Boundary neuron gates (mediators between regions)
        self.conf_to_treat_gate = nn.Sequential(
            nn.Linear(2*hidden_dim, 1),
            nn.Sigmoid()
        )
        self.treat_to_outc_gate = nn.Sequential(
            nn.Linear(2*hidden_dim, 1),
            nn.Sigmoid()
        )

        # Subgraph processors using heterogeneous convolution
        self.conf_conv = HeteroConv({
            ('confounder', 'affects', 'confounder'):
            ↪   GATConv(hidden_dim, hidden_dim, num_heads,
            ↪   concat=False),
            ('confounder', 'influences', 'treatment'):
            ↪   SAGEConv(hidden_dim, hidden_dim)
        }, aggr='mean')

        self.treat_conv = HeteroConv({
            ('treatment', 'impacts', 'outcome'): GATConv(hidden_dim,
            ↪   hidden_dim, num_heads, concat=False)
```

186

```
    }, aggr='max')

    # Structural equation model for outcomes
    self.structural_eq = nn.Sequential(
        nn.Linear(2*hidden_dim, hidden_dim),
        nn.ReLU(),
        nn.Linear(hidden_dim, 1)
    )

def forward(self, data: HeteroData):
    # Initial feature projection
    x_conf = self.conf_encoder(data['confounder'].x)
    x_treat = self.treat_encoder(data['treatment'].x)
    x_outc = self.outc_encoder(data['outcome'].x)

    # Confounder subgraph processing
    conf_edge_index = data['confounder', 'affects',
    ↪ 'confounder'].edge_index
    treat_edge_index = data['confounder', 'influences',
    ↪ 'treatment'].edge_index

    # Phase 1: Confounder region message passing
    conf_out = self.conf_conv(
        {'confounder': x_conf},
        {'confounder': {'affects': conf_edge_index},
         'treatment': {'influences': treat_edge_index}}
    )

    # Boundary mediation: Confounder → Treatment
    boundary_mask = data['confounder', 'influences',
    ↪ 'treatment'].edge_index
    src, dst = boundary_mask
    gate_input = torch.cat([x_conf[src], x_treat[dst]], dim=-1)
    gate_values = self.conf_to_treat_gate(gate_input).squeeze()

    # Aggregate gate values per treatment node
    gate_per_treat = scatter_mean(gate_values, dst, dim=0,
    ↪ dim_size=x_treat.size(0))
    x_treat = x_treat + gate_per_treat.unsqueeze(-1) *
    ↪ conf_out['treatment']

    # Phase 2: Treatment subgraph processing
    treat_out = self.treat_conv(
        {'treatment': x_treat},
        {'outcome': {'impacts': data['treatment', 'impacts',
         ↪ 'outcome'].edge_index}}
    )

    # Boundary mediation: Treatment → Outcome
    outc_edge_index = data['treatment', 'impacts',
    ↪ 'outcome'].edge_index
    src, dst = outc_edge_index
    gate_input = torch.cat([x_treat[src], x_outc[dst]], dim=-1)
```

```python
        gate_values = self.treat_to_outc_gate(gate_input).squeeze()

        # Aggregate gate values per outcome node
        gate_per_outc = scatter_mean(gate_values, dst, dim=0,
        ↪    dim_size=x_outc.size(0))
        x_outc = x_outc + gate_per_outc.unsqueeze(-1) *
        ↪    treat_out['outcome']

        # Phase 3: Structural equation modeling
        conf_outc_edges = data['confounder', 'affects',
        ↪    'outcome'].edge_index
        conf_features = x_conf[conf_outc_edges[0]]
        outc_features = x_outc[conf_outc_edges[1]]
        structural_input = torch.cat([conf_features, outc_features],
        ↪    dim=-1)

        # Final outcome prediction
        potential_outcomes = self.structural_eq(structural_input)
        return potential_outcomes.squeeze()

class CausalGraphDataset:
    """Generates synthetic heterogeneous graphs for causal
    ↪    analysis"""
    def __init__(self, num_samples=1000):
        self.num_samples = num_samples
        self.node_types = ['confounder', 'treatment', 'outcome']

    def _generate_graph(self):
        data = HeteroData()

        # Confounder nodes (age, income, education)
        data['confounder'].x = torch.randn(50, 10)
        data['confounder', 'affects', 'confounder'].edge_index =
        ↪    self._sparse_edges(50, 0.1)

        # Treatment nodes (medical interventions)
        data['treatment'].x = torch.randn(20, 5)
        conf_treat_edges = torch.stack([
            torch.randint(0, 50, (30,)),
            torch.randint(0, 20, (30,))
        ], dim=0)
        data['confounder', 'influences', 'treatment'].edge_index =
        ↪    conf_treat_edges

        # Outcome nodes (health results)
        data['outcome'].x = torch.randn(10, 3)
        treat_outc_edges = torch.stack([
            torch.randint(0, 20, (15,)),
            torch.randint(0, 10, (15,))
        ], dim=0)
        data['treatment', 'impacts', 'outcome'].edge_index =
        ↪    treat_outc_edges
```

```python
        conf_outc_edges = torch.stack([
            torch.randint(0, 50, (20,)),
            torch.randint(0, 10, (20,))
        ], dim=0)
        data['confounder', 'affects', 'outcome'].edge_index =
        ↪    conf_outc_edges

        return data

    def _sparse_edges(self, num_nodes, density):
        mask = torch.rand(num_nodes, num_nodes) < density
        return mask.nonzero(as_tuple=False).t()

    def __getitem__(self, idx):
        return self._generate_graph()


def causal_loss(pred, target, model, alpha=0.5):
    """Loss combining prediction error and boundary
    ↪    regularization"""
    mse_loss = F.mse_loss(pred, target)

    # Boundary activation regularization
    gate_activations = torch.cat([
        model.conf_to_treat_gate[0].weight.view(-1),
        model.treat_to_outc_gate[0].weight.view(-1)
    ])
    reg_loss = torch.norm(gate_activations, p=1)

    return mse_loss + alpha * reg_loss


def train_nbhge():
    device = torch.device('cuda' if torch.cuda.is_available() else
    ↪    'cpu')
    dataset = CausalGraphDataset(num_samples=100)
    model = NBHGE(hidden_dim=64).to(device)
    optimizer = torch.optim.Adam(model.parameters(), lr=0.001)

    for epoch in range(1, 101):
        total_loss = 0
        for _ in range(len(dataset)):
            data = dataset[0].to(device)
            optimizer.zero_grad()

            # Synthetic targets (simulated outcomes)
            pred = model(data)
            target = torch.randn_like(pred)

            loss = causal_loss(pred, target, model)
            loss.backward()
            optimizer.step()
            total_loss += loss.item()

        if epoch % 10 == 0:
```

```
        print(f'Epoch {epoch:03d} | Loss:
        ↪  {total_loss/len(dataset):.4f}')

if __name__ == "__main__":
    train_nbhge()
```

Key Implementation Details:

- **Region Partitioning:** The `NBHGE` class explicitly separates confounder, treatment, and outcome regions using PyG's heterogeneous graph format. Each region maintains distinct feature encoders (`conf_encoder`, `treat_encoder`, `outc_encoder`).

- **Boundary Neurons:** Trainable gating mechanisms (`conf_to_treat_gate`, `treat_to_outc_gate`) mediate inter-region communication. These gates combine source and destination features to compute weighted interaction coefficients.

- **Directed Message Passing:** The `HeteroConv` layers enforce region-specific propagation rules. Confounder-to-treatment edges use SageConv for neighborhood aggregation, while treatment-to-outcome edges employ GATConv for attention-weighted impacts.

- **Structural Equations:** The `structural_eq` module combines confounder and outcome features to estimate potential outcomes, modeling the final causal relationship through learnable nonlinear transformations.

- **Regularized Training:** The `causal_loss` function combines prediction error with L1 regularization on boundary gate weights, encouraging sparse interpretable connections between subgraphs.

- **Synthetic Graph Generation:** The `CausalGraphDataset` creates heterogeneous graphs with realistic connection patterns between regions, including confounder-confounder edges and bipartite treatment-outcome links.

- **Counterfactual Readout:** Model outputs represent potential outcomes under different treatment scenarios, enabling what-if analysis through targeted feature perturbation in the treatment region.

190

Chapter 27

Online and Incremental Learning with NBHGE

This chapter implements continuous learning for dynamic graphs using the Neuron-Boundary Heterogeneous Graph Engine (NBHGE). Our architecture maintains adaptable boundary neurons that mediate between stable regions while incrementally integrating new data patterns. The system preserves existing knowledge through selective retraining and structural updates.

Key implementation strategy:

- Initialize graph partitions with boundary neuron interfaces between regions

- Process data streams through three-phase updates:

    - **Stable Region Preservation:** Freeze embeddings for mature subgraphs with consistent patterns

    - **Boundary Adjustment:** Update interface neurons between regions using restricted attention windows

    - **Novelty Handling:** Create new partitions with fresh boundary neurons for unrecognized patterns

- Maintain dual update modes:

    - Incremental edge updates through adjacency matrix patches

    - Full partition instantiation for significant distribution shifts

- Implement memory-aware training that prioritizes boundary neuron retraining

Python Code Snippet

```python
import torch
import torch.nn as nn
import torch.nn.functional as F
from collections import defaultdict
import numpy as np
from sklearn.metrics import pairwise_distances

class NBHGEngine(nn.Module):
    """
    Neuron-Boundary Heterogeneous Graph Engine
    Implements incremental learning through boundary neuron
    ↪ mediation
    and dynamic graph partitioning
    """
    def __init__(self, num_node_types, embed_dim=128,
                    boundary_threshold=0.35, max_regions=10):
        super().__init__()
        self.embed_dim = embed_dim
        self.boundary_threshold = boundary_threshold
        self.max_regions = max_regions

        # Core NBHGE components
        self.node_embeddings = nn.ParameterDict()
        self.boundary_neurons = nn.ParameterList()
        self.region_partitions = defaultdict(set)
        self.adjacency_matrices = defaultdict(lambda:
        ↪ defaultdict(set))

        # Region-specific parameters
        self.region_projectors = nn.ModuleDict()
        self.region_classifiers = nn.ModuleDict()

        # Incremental learning buffers
        self.pending_edges = defaultdict(list)
        self.candidate_boundaries = defaultdict(set)

        # Initialize first region
        self._create_new_region('initial_region')

    def _create_new_region(self, region_id):
        """Establish new graph partition with boundary interface"""
        # Initialize region-specific parameters
        self.region_projectors[region_id] = nn.Sequential(
            nn.Linear(self.embed_dim, self.embed_dim//2),
            nn.GELU(),
```

```python
        nn.LayerNorm(self.embed_dim//2)
    )
    self.region_classifiers[region_id] = nn.Linear(
        self.embed_dim//2, num_node_types
    )

    # Add boundary neuron between new and previous regions
    if len(self.boundary_neurons) > 0:
        boundary_weight = nn.Parameter(
            torch.randn(self.embed_dim, self.embed_dim)
        )
        self.boundary_neurons.append(boundary_weight)

    print(f"Created new region partition: {region_id}")

def register_node(self, node_id, node_type, initial_embed=None):
    """Add node to appropriate region with type-aware
    ↪ embedding"""
    if initial_embed is None:
        initial_embed = torch.randn(self.embed_dim)

    # Store node in most compatible existing region
    if len(self.node_embeddings) > 0:
        existing_nodes = list(self.node_embeddings.keys())
        existing_embeds =
        ↪ torch.stack(list(self.node_embeddings.values()))
        similarities = F.cosine_similarity(initial_embed,
        ↪ existing_embeds)
        most_similar_idx = similarities.argmax().item()
        most_similar_node = existing_nodes[most_similar_idx]

        target_region = None
        for region, nodes in self.region_partitions.items():
            if most_similar_node in nodes:
                target_region = region
                break
        if target_region is None:
            target_region = 'initial_region'
    else:
        target_region = 'initial_region'

    self.node_embeddings[node_id] = nn.Parameter(initial_embed)
    self.region_partitions[target_region].add(node_id)

def add_edge(self, src_node, dest_node, edge_type):
    """Queue edge for incremental adjacency update"""
    self.pending_edges[edge_type].append((src_node, dest_node))

def _update_boundary_neurons(self, region_pairs, lr=0.01):
    """Adjust boundary interfaces between specified regions"""
    with torch.no_grad():
        for (src_region, dest_region) in region_pairs:
            if not self.boundary_neurons:
```

```
        continue

    # Find valid boundary index
    try:
        src_num = int(src_region.split('_')[-1]) if
        ↪   src_region != 'initial_region' else 0
        dest_num = int(dest_region.split('_')[-1]) if
        ↪   dest_region != 'initial_region' else 0
        boundary_idx = min(src_num, dest_num) - 1
        if boundary_idx < 0 or boundary_idx >=
        ↪   len(self.boundary_neurons):
            boundary_idx =
            ↪   min(len(self.boundary_neurons)-1, max(0,
            ↪   len(self.region_partitions)-2))
    except:
        boundary_idx = min(len(self.boundary_neurons)-1,
        ↪   max(0, len(self.region_partitions)-2))

    if boundary_idx < 0 or boundary_idx >=
    ↪   len(self.boundary_neurons):
        continue

    W = self.boundary_neurons[boundary_idx]

    # Calculate alignment loss between regions
    src_embeds = torch.stack([
        self.node_embeddings[n]
        for n in self.region_partitions[src_region]
    ]) if self.region_partitions[src_region] else
    ↪   torch.zeros(0, self.embed_dim)

    dest_embeds = torch.stack([
        self.node_embeddings[n]
        for n in self.region_partitions[dest_region]
    ]) if self.region_partitions[dest_region] else
    ↪   torch.zeros(0, self.embed_dim)

    if src_embeds.numel() == 0 or dest_embeds.numel() ==
    ↪   0:
        continue

    # Boundary neuron update rule with mean alignment
    transformed_src = src_embeds @ W
    mean_src = transformed_src.mean(dim=0)
    mean_dest = dest_embeds.mean(dim=0)
    alignment_loss = torch.norm(mean_src - mean_dest,
    ↪   p=2)

    # Manual gradient calculation and update
    grad_W = torch.autograd.grad(alignment_loss, W,
    ↪   retain_graph=True)[0]
    W.data -= lr * grad_W
```

```python
def _detect_distribution_shift(self, new_embeds):
    """Identify novel patterns requiring new regions"""
    if len(self.node_embeddings) == 0:
        return True

    existing = torch.stack(list(self.node_embeddings.values()))
    distances = pairwise_distances(
        new_embeds.cpu().numpy(),
        existing.detach().cpu().numpy(),
        metric='cosine'
    )
    return np.mean(distances) > self.boundary_threshold

def incremental_step(self, batch_nodes, batch_edges):
    """Process new data batch with NBHGE update rules"""
    # Phase 1: Node registration and novelty detection
    new_embeds = torch.stack([n[2] for n in batch_nodes])
    if self._detect_distribution_shift(new_embeds):
        if len(self.region_partitions) < self.max_regions:
            new_region = f'region_{len(self.region_partitions)}'
            self._create_new_region(new_region)

    # Register new nodes with type embeddings
    for node_id, node_type, embed in batch_nodes:
        self.register_node(node_id, node_type, embed)

    # Phase 2: Edge processing with boundary tracking
    for edge_type, edges in batch_edges.items():
        for src, dest in edges:
            self.add_edge(src, dest, edge_type)

            # Detect cross-region connections for boundary
            ↪  attention
            src_region = next(
                r for r, nodes in self.region_partitions.items()
                if src in nodes
            )
            dest_region = next(
                r for r, nodes in self.region_partitions.items()
                if dest in nodes
            )
            if src_region != dest_region:
                self.candidate_boundaries[(src_region,
                ↪  dest_region)].update(
                    {src, dest}
                )

    # Process pending edges into adjacency matrices
    for edge_type, edges in self.pending_edges.items():
        for src, dest in edges:
            self.adjacency_matrices[edge_type][src].add(dest)
            self.adjacency_matrices[edge_type][dest].add(src)
    self.pending_edges.clear()
```

```python
    # Phase 3: Selective boundary neuron updates
    region_pairs = list(self.candidate_boundaries.keys())
    if len(region_pairs) > 0:
        self._update_boundary_neurons(region_pairs)

    # Phase 4: Stability-preserving parameter updates
    for region_id in self.region_partitions:
        if region_id not in [pair[0] for pair in region_pairs]:
            # Freeze stable regions not involved in boundary
            ↪ updates
            for node in self.region_partitions[region_id]:
                self.node_embeddings[node].requires_grad_(False)

def forward(self, node_ids):
    """Execute cross-region information propagation"""
    embeds = torch.stack([self.node_embeddings[n] for n in
    ↪ node_ids])

    # Apply region-specific projection
    region_embeds = {}
    region_nodes_dict = {}
    for region, nodes in self.region_partitions.items():
        region_nodes = [n for n in node_ids if n in nodes]
        if len(region_nodes) > 0:
            region_idx = [node_ids.index(n) for n in
            ↪ region_nodes]
            proj =
            ↪ self.region_projectors[region](embeds[region_idx])
            region_embeds[region] = proj
            region_nodes_dict[region] = region_nodes

    # Boundary neuron mediation
    final_embeds = torch.zeros_like(embeds)
    for i, node_id in enumerate(node_ids):
        home_region = next(
            r for r, nodes in self.region_partitions.items()
            if node_id in nodes
        )
        # Get region-specific embedding
        region_nodes = region_nodes_dict.get(home_region, [])
        if node_id in region_nodes:
            node_index = region_nodes.index(node_id)
            final_embeds[i] =
            ↪ region_embeds[home_region][node_index]

        # Apply boundary transformations for cross-region
        ↪ connections
        for boundary_idx, (src_reg, dest_reg) in
        ↪ enumerate(self.candidate_boundaries.keys()):
            if boundary_idx < len(self.boundary_neurons) and
            ↪ home_region == src_reg:
                boundary_W = self.boundary_neurons[boundary_idx]
```

196

```python
            final_embeds[i] = final_embeds[i] @ boundary_W

        return final_embeds

class StreamingGraphDataset:
    """Simulates continuous graph data stream"""
    def __init__(self, node_types, embed_dim=128):
        self.node_types = node_types
        self.embed_dim = embed_dim
        self.current_batch = 0

    def generate_batch(self, batch_size=32):
        # Simulate new nodes and edges
        new_nodes = [
            (f"node_{self.current_batch}_{i}",
             np.random.choice(self.node_types),
             torch.randn(self.embed_dim))
            for i in range(batch_size)
        ]

        new_edges = defaultdict(list)
        for _ in range(batch_size//2):
            src =
            ↪ f"node_{self.current_batch}_{np.random.randint(batch_size)}"
            dest =
            ↪ f"node_{self.current_batch}_{np.random.randint(batch_size)}"
            new_edges['interaction'].append((src, dest))

        self.current_batch += 1
        return new_nodes, new_edges

def online_training_loop(model, dataset, num_steps=100):
    """Continuous learning process with NBHGE"""
    optimizer = torch.optim.AdamW(model.parameters(), lr=1e-3)

    for step in range(num_steps):
        nodes, edges = dataset.generate_batch()
        model.incremental_step(nodes, edges)

        # Selective boundary-aware optimization
        active_regions = set(
            [r for pair in model.candidate_boundaries
             for r in pair]
        )
        if len(active_regions) > 0:
            optimizer.param_groups[0]['params'] = [
                p for n,p in model.named_parameters()
                if any(r in n for r in active_regions)
            ]
            optimizer.step()
            optimizer.zero_grad()

def main():
```

```
# Initialize NBHGE with 3 node types (users, items, contexts)
model = NBHGEngine(num_node_types=3)
dataset = StreamingGraphDataset(node_types=['user', 'item',
↪  'context'])

# Run continuous learning process
online_training_loop(model, dataset, num_steps=50)

# Inspect final region partitions
print("\nFinal region configuration:")
for region, nodes in model.region_partitions.items():
    print(f"{region}: {len(nodes)} nodes")

print("Boundary neurons count:", len(model.boundary_neurons))

if __name__ == "__main__":
    main()
```

Key Implementation Details:

- **Boundary Neuron Mechanics:** The `_update_boundary_neurons` method implements alignment loss minimization between connected regions, adjusting projection matrices that mediate inter-region communication while preserving intra-region stability.

- **Incremental Processing Pipeline:** The `incremental_step` method orchestrates the four-phase update sequence: node registration, edge processing, boundary adjustment, and stability preservation through parameter freezing.

- **Novelty Detection:** The `_detect_distribution_shift` method uses cosine similarity thresholds to trigger new region creation when encountering significantly different node embeddings.

- **Selective Backpropagation:** The training loop dynamically adjusts optimizer parameters to only update weights associated with active boundary regions, dramatically reducing computational overhead.

- **Cross-Region Propagation:** The `forward` method implements boundary-aware feature transformation, applying learned projection matrices only when information crosses between partitions.

198

- **Memory Management:** Region partitions track node memberships while pending edges buffer temporary connections until boundary analysis completes, preventing premature graph modifications.

- **Stability-Preservation:** Mature regions have their node embeddings frozen via `requires_grad_(False)` when not involved in recent boundary updates, maintaining stable representations.

Chapter 28

Neuro-Symbolic Reasoning for Structured Data

This chapter implements a Neuron-Boundary Heterogeneous Graph Engine (NBHGE) that synergizes neural graph networks with symbolic reasoning through adaptive boundary neurons. The architecture establishes two distinct processing regions connected by learned boundary interfaces that translate between continuous embeddings and discrete logic constraints.

- Define heterogeneous graph structure with typed nodes and relationships

- Partition graph into two computational regions:

  - **Symbolic Region:** Handles logic rules and constraint satisfaction through differentiable operations

  - **Neural Region:** Processes node embeddings via graph attention networks

- Implement boundary neurons as trainable interfaces between regions:

  - Convert symbolic constraints to embedding-space gradients

  - Project neural activations into rule satisfaction probabilities

- Jointly optimize embedding quality and rule adherence through boundary-mediated loss

- Enable bidirectional adaptation between neural patterns and symbolic knowledge

Python Code Snippet

```python
import torch
import torch.nn as nn
import torch.nn.functional as F
from torch_geometric.nn import GATConv
from torch_geometric.data import Data
import numpy as np


# ------------------------------------------------------------
# Neuron-Boundary Heterogeneous Graph Engine (NBHGE)
# ------------------------------------------------------------
class NBHGEModel(nn.Module):
    """
    Neuro-symbolic graph model with:
    - Neural Region: GAT-based node embedding network
    - Symbolic Region: Differentiable logic rule evaluator
    - Boundary Neurons: Bidirectional interface layers
    """

    def __init__(self, num_nodes, node_dim, rule_dim, boundary_dim):
        super().__init__()

        # Neural Region Components
        self.gat1 = GATConv(node_dim, 64, heads=4)
        self.gat2 = GATConv(64*4, 128)
        self.node_proj = nn.Linear(128, node_dim)

        # Symbolic Rule Components
        self.rule_embeddings = nn.Embedding(num_nodes, rule_dim)
        self.rule_fc = nn.Sequential(
            nn.Linear(rule_dim, 64),
            nn.ReLU(),
            nn.Linear(64, rule_dim)
        )

        # Boundary Interface
        self.boundary_n2r = nn.Linear(node_dim, boundary_dim)  #
        ↪  Neural to rule
        self.boundary_r2n = nn.Linear(rule_dim, boundary_dim)  #
        ↪  Rule to neural
        self.boundary_gate = nn.Parameter(torch.randn(boundary_dim))

        # Output Layers
```

```python
        self.classifier = nn.Linear(node_dim + 1, 1)  # Adjusted
        ↪   input dimension

def forward(self, data, rules):
    """
    Process both neural and symbolic regions with boundary
    ↪   mediation
    data: PyG Data object with edge_index and node features
    rules: Tensor of shape [num_rules, 3] (head, relation, tail)
    """
    # --------------- Neural Region Processing ---------------
    x, edge_index = data.x, data.edge_index

    # First GAT layer with expanded dimensionality
    x = F.elu(self.gat1(x, edge_index))
    x = F.dropout(x, p=0.3, training=self.training)

    # Second GAT layer with feature compression
    x = F.elu(self.gat2(x, edge_index))
    neural_out = self.node_proj(x)

    # --------------- Symbolic Region Processing ---------------
    # Get rule component embeddings
    rule_heads = self.rule_embeddings(rules[:,0])
    rule_relations =
    ↪   self.rule_fc(self.rule_embeddings(rules[:,1]))
    rule_tails = self.rule_embeddings(rules[:,2])

    # Calculate rule satisfaction scores (transE-style)
    symbolic_out = torch.norm(
        rule_heads + rule_relations - rule_tails,
        p=2, dim=-1, keepdim=True
    )

    # --------------- Boundary Mediation ---------------
    # Neural to Symbolic translation
    neural_boundary = self.boundary_n2r(neural_out)
    neural_boundary = F.glu(neural_boundary *
    ↪   self.boundary_gate)

    # Symbolic to Neural translation
    symbolic_boundary = self.boundary_r2n(rule_heads)
    symbolic_boundary = symbolic_boundary.mean(dim=0)
    symbolic_boundary = F.glu(symbolic_boundary *
    ↪   self.boundary_gate)

    # Adaptive fusion
    neural_out = neural_out + symbolic_boundary.unsqueeze(1)
    symbolic_out = symbolic_out +
    ↪   neural_boundary.mean(1).unsqueeze(-1)

    # --------------- Joint Prediction ---------------
    combined = torch.cat([
```

```
                neural_out[rules[:,0]],
                symbolic_out
            ], dim=-1)

        return torch.sigmoid(self.classifier(combined)).squeeze()

# ---------------------------------------------------------------
# Training Infrastructure
# ---------------------------------------------------------------
class NeuroSymbolicDataset:
    """Combines graph data and symbolic rules"""
    def __init__(self, graph_data, rule_set):
        self.graph = graph_data
        self.rules = rule_set  # Tensor of shape [num_rules, 3]

    def __len__(self):
        return 1  # Single instance containing full graph and rules

    def __getitem__(self, idx):
        return self.graph, self.rules

def create_boundary_loss(predictions, graph_data, alpha=0.7):
    """
    Hybrid loss combining:
    - Prediction cross-entropy (30%)
    - Neural embedding quality (40%)
    - Rule consistency (30%)
    """
    # Prediction loss
    ce_loss = F.binary_cross_entropy(predictions,
    ↪  graph_data.y.float())

    # Neural embedding regularization
    embeddings = graph_data.x
    emb_loss = torch.mean(torch.var(embeddings, dim=0))  # Prevent
    ↪  collapse

    # Rule consistency enforcement
    rule_loss = torch.mean(predictions * torch.log(predictions +
    ↪  1e-8))

    return alpha*ce_loss + (1-alpha)*(emb_loss - 0.5*rule_loss)

def train_nbhge(model, dataset, epochs=100, lr=0.001):
    optimizer = torch.optim.AdamW(model.parameters(), lr=lr)
    for epoch in range(epochs):
        total_loss = 0
        for graph, rules in dataset:
            optimizer.zero_grad()
            preds = model(graph, rules)
            loss = create_boundary_loss(preds, graph)
            loss.backward()
            optimizer.step()
```

```
            total_loss += loss.item()
        print(f"Epoch {epoch+1} | Loss:
        ↪ {total_loss/len(dataset):.4f}")

# ------------------------------------------------------------
# Example Usage
# ------------------------------------------------------------
if __name__ == "__main__":
    # Sample knowledge graph data
    edge_index = torch.tensor([[0,1,2,0], [1,2,0,2]],
    ↪ dtype=torch.long)
    node_features = torch.randn(3, 64)  # 3 nodes with 64-dim
    ↪ features
    graph_data = Data(x=node_features, edge_index=edge_index,
    ↪ y=torch.tensor([1.0, 0.0]))

    # Sample symbolic rules (head, relation, tail)
    rules = torch.tensor([[0,1,2], [2,0,1]], dtype=torch.long)

    # Initialize NBHGE model
    model = NBHGEModel(
        num_nodes=3,
        node_dim=64,
        rule_dim=32,
        boundary_dim=48
    )

    # Create dataset and train
    dataset = NeuroSymbolicDataset(graph_data, rules)
    train_nbhge(model, dataset, epochs=50)
```

Key Implementation Details:

- **Boundary Neuron Mechanics:** The `boundary_n2r` and `boundary_r2n` layers implement learnable translation spaces between neural embeddings and symbolic rule representations. The gated GLU activation enables non-linear, context-aware signal modulation.

- **Dual-Region Processing:** Neural region uses stacked GAT layers with ELU activations for neighborhood aggregation, while symbolic region employs TransE-style distance metrics over learned rule embeddings.

- **Adaptive Fusion:** Boundary outputs modify both regions through residual connections, allowing neural embeddings to absorb symbolic constraints while rule representations adapt to learned patterns.

204

- **Hybrid Loss Function:** The `create_boundary_loss` combines prediction accuracy, embedding variance maximization (prevent collapse), and rule consistency enforcement through entropy maximization.

- **Bi-directional Translation:** Boundary neurons operate in both directions - projecting neural activations into rule satisfaction gradients while injecting symbolic constraints into embedding updates.

- **Unified Parameter Space:** All components including GAT layers, rule embeddings, and boundary interfaces are jointly optimized through gradient descent, enabling end-to-end neuro-symbolic reasoning.

Chapter 29

Graph Summarization and Simplification

This chapter implements graph compression through the Neuron-Boundary Heterogeneous Graph Engine (NBHGE), which reduces graph complexity while preserving structural patterns. The system identifies dense node clusters, establishes boundary neurons as inter-region mediators, and iteratively merges similar nodes into super-nodes represented by these boundary units.

Key implementation steps:

- Initialize heterogeneous graph with node features and connection weights

- Detect dense partitions using modularity optimization with boundary constraints

- Calculate similarity scores between nodes using feature and topological metrics

- Merge nodes exceeding similarity thresholds into super-nodes

- Update boundary neurons to handle inter-region communication

- Recalculate embeddings for merged nodes using neighborhood aggregation

- Repeat summarization process across multiple hierarchy levels

- Maintain connection history for traceability through compression layers

Python Code Snippet

```python
import torch
import torch.nn as nn
import torch.nn.functional as F
from torch_geometric.data import Data
from torch_geometric.nn import MessagePassing
from torch_scatter import scatter_mean
import networkx as nx
from sklearn.metrics.pairwise import cosine_similarity
from collections import defaultdict

# ------------------------------------------------------------
# Core NBHGE Components
# ------------------------------------------------------------
class BoundaryNeuron(nn.Module):
    '''
    Mediates information flow between graph partitions
    Maintains connections to both internal cluster nodes and
    ↪ external boundaries
    '''

    def __init__(self, embed_dim):
        super().__init__()
        self.interface_weights = nn.Parameter(torch.randn(embed_dim,
        ↪ embed_dim))
        self.memory_gate = nn.Linear(2*embed_dim, embed_dim)

    def forward(self, internal_embeds, external_embeds):
        # Transform internal features to boundary space
        transformed_internal = torch.mm(internal_embeds,
        ↪ self.interface_weights)

        # Concatenate with external context
        combined = torch.cat([transformed_internal,
        ↪ external_embeds], dim=-1)

        # Gated memory update
        gate = torch.sigmoid(self.memory_gate(combined))
        return gate * transformed_internal + (1 - gate) *
        ↪ external_embeds

class NBHGE(MessagePassing):
    '''
    Neuron-Boundary Heterogeneous Graph Engine
    Implements multi-level graph summarization through:
    - Adaptive boundary neuron placement
    - Similarity-driven node merging
```

```
    - Hierarchical embedding propagation
    '''
    def __init__(self, embed_dim=128, merge_threshold=0.85,
            max_partition_size=50, num_hops=3):
        super().__init__(aggr='mean')
        self.merge_threshold = merge_threshold
        self.max_partition_size = max_partition_size
        self.boundaries = nn.ModuleDict()
        self.node_registry = defaultdict(dict)

        # Shared projection for feature alignment
        self.feature_projector = nn.Sequential(
            nn.Linear(embed_dim, 2*embed_dim),
            nn.ReLU(),
            nn.Linear(2*embed_dim, embed_dim)
        )

    def initialize_partitions(self, data):
        '''Create initial graph partitions using modularity
        ↪    optimization'''
        G = nx.Graph(data.edge_index.numpy().T)
        partition = nx.community.greedy_modularity_communities(G)

        # Create boundary neurons for each partition
        self.boundaries.clear()
        for i, comm in enumerate(partition):
            boundary_id = f'boundary_{i}'
            self.boundaries[boundary_id] =
            ↪    BoundaryNeuron(data.num_features)

            # Register nodes with their boundary
            for node_id in comm:
                self.node_registry[node_id] = {
                    'boundary': boundary_id,
                    'active': True
                }

        return self._create_updated_graph(data)

    def _create_updated_graph(self, original_data):
        '''Generate compressed graph with boundary nodes'''
        # Aggregate features for active nodes
        active_nodes = [n for n, meta in self.node_registry.items()
        ↪    if meta['active']]
        compressed_features = original_data.x[active_nodes]

        # Add boundary node features
        boundary_features = [bn.interface_weights.mean(dim=0)
                        for bn in self.boundaries.values()]
        all_features = torch.cat([compressed_features,
                            torch.stack(boundary_features)])

        # Rebuild edge index with boundary connections
```

208

```python
        edge_list = self._reconnect_edges(original_data.edge_index,
        ↪   active_nodes)

        return Data(x=all_features, edge_index=edge_list)

    def _reconnect_edges(self, original_edges, active_nodes):
        '''Reconstruct edges considering merged nodes and
        ↪   boundaries'''
        new_edges = []
        num_active = len(active_nodes)
        boundary_list = list(self.boundaries.keys())

        for src, dst in original_edges.t().tolist():
            src_meta = self.node_registry.get(src, {'active': False,
            ↪   'boundary': None})
            dst_meta = self.node_registry.get(dst, {'active': False,
            ↪   'boundary': None})

            # Handle active node connections
            if src_meta['active'] and dst_meta['active']:
                new_edges.append([src, dst])

            # Connect to boundary if either node was merged
            elif src_meta['active']:
                if dst_meta['boundary'] in boundary_list:
                    boundary_id =
                    ↪   boundary_list.index(dst_meta['boundary'])
                    new_edges.append([src, num_active +
                    ↪   boundary_id])

            elif dst_meta['active']:
                if src_meta['boundary'] in boundary_list:
                    boundary_id =
                    ↪   boundary_list.index(src_meta['boundary'])
                    new_edges.append([num_active + boundary_id,
                    ↪   dst])

        return torch.tensor(new_edges).t().contiguous()

    def merge_nodes(self, data):
        '''Identify and merge similar nodes within partitions'''
        similarity_matrix =
        ↪   cosine_similarity(data.x.detach().numpy())
        merged_pairs = []

        # Find merge candidates within each partition
        for boundary_id, bn in self.boundaries.items():
            node_ids = [n for n, meta in self.node_registry.items()
                        if meta['boundary'] == boundary_id and
                        ↪   meta['active']]

            # Check pairwise similarities
            for i in range(len(node_ids)):
```

```python
            for j in range(i+1, len(node_ids)):
                if similarity_matrix[node_ids[i], node_ids[j]] >
                ↪  self.merge_threshold:
                    merged_pairs.append((node_ids[i],
                    ↪  node_ids[j]))

        # Process merges and update registry
        new_features = []
        for src, dst in merged_pairs:
            if self.node_registry[src]['active'] and
            ↪  self.node_registry[dst]['active']:
                # Mark nodes as merged
                self.node_registry[src]['active'] = False
                self.node_registry[dst]['active'] = False

                # Create new super-node
                new_id = len(data.x) + len(new_features)
                self.node_registry[new_id] = {
                    'boundary': self.node_registry[src]['boundary'],
                    'active': True
                }

                # Collect merged features
                new_features.append((data.x[src] + data.x[dst]) / 2)

        # Update data with merged nodes
        if new_features:
            data.x = torch.cat([data.x, torch.stack(new_features)],
            ↪  dim=0)

        return self._create_updated_graph(data)

    def forward(self, data, num_iters=3):
        '''Execute multi-iteration summarization'''
        compressed_data = self.initialize_partitions(data)
        for _ in range(num_iters):
            compressed_data = self.merge_nodes(compressed_data)
            compressed_data.x =
            ↪  self.feature_projector(compressed_data.x)
        return compressed_data


# ------------------------------------------------------------
# Implementation Utilities
# ------------------------------------------------------------
def create_sample_graph():
    '''Create synthetic social network graph with user cliques'''
    edge_index = torch.tensor([[0,1,1,2,2,0,3,4,4,5,5,3,0,3,2,4],
                               [1,2,0,0,1,2,4,5,3,3,4,5,3,0,4,2]],
                              ↪  dtype=torch.long)
    x = torch.randn(6, 128)  # User feature vectors
    return Data(x=x, edge_index=edge_index)


# ------------------------------------------------------------
```

```
# Execution Pipeline
# ----------------------------------------------------------------
def main():
    # Initialize NBHGE with compression parameters
    summarizer = NBHGE(merge_threshold=0.8, max_partition_size=25)

    # Generate sample social network graph
    original_graph = create_sample_graph()
    print(f"Original graph: {original_graph.num_nodes} nodes, "
          f"{original_graph.num_edges} edges")

    # Perform 3-level summarization
    compressed_graph = summarizer(original_graph, num_iters=3)
    print(f"Compressed graph: {compressed_graph.num_nodes} nodes, "
          f"{compressed_graph.num_edges} edges")

if __name__ == "__main__":
    main()
```

Key Implementation Details:

- **Boundary Neuron Mechanics:** The `BoundaryNeuron` class implements gated information fusion between internal cluster features and external context using learnable interface weights and memory gates.

- **Adaptive Partitioning:** The `initialize_partitions` method uses modularity optimization to detect natural community structures while respecting maximum partition size constraints.

- **Similarity-Driven Merging:** The `merge_nodes` method identifies merge candidates using cosine similarity thresholds and creates super-nodes with averaged embeddings while updating boundary associations.

- **Dynamic Edge Reconstruction:** The `_reconnect_edges` method preserves connectivity patterns by redirecting edges to boundary neurons when original nodes are merged.

- **Hierarchical Feature Propagation:** Multiple summarization iterations in the `forward` method enable progressive compression, with feature projection layers aligning embeddings across hierarchy levels.

- **Memory-Efficient Representation:** The node registry system tracks active/merged status and boundary associations without modifying original graph data structures.

- **Topology Preservation:** Boundary neurons maintain inter-region connectivity through learned interface transformations, preserving structural patterns despite node reductions.

Chapter 30

Counterfactual Reasoning Using Boundary Neuron Graph Partitioning

This chapter implements counterfactual reasoning through Neuron-Boundary Heterogeneous Graph Engine (NBHGE) architecture. Our approach enables systematic exploration of alternative scenarios by manipulating boundary neurons that mediate information flow between graph partitions. The system learns to project localized graph modifications through specialized boundary units while maintaining global consistency.

Key implementation steps:

- Construct heterogeneous graph with multimodal node/edge attributes

- Partition graph into regions using modularity-based community detection

- Initialize boundary neurons at partition interfaces with gating mechanisms

- Implement counterfactual transformations through:

    - Boundary neuron activation masking

- Subgraph feature/value substitutions
- Edge existence toggling with dependency propagation

- Compute factual/counterfactual outcome divergence

- Optimize boundary neuron positions for maximal intervention impact

Python Code Snippet

```python
import torch
import torch.nn as nn
import torch.nn.functional as F
import numpy as np
import networkx as nx
from torch_geometric.data import Data
from torch_geometric.nn import GCNConv, HeteroConv
from sklearn.metrics import pairwise_distances
from community import community_louvain


# ----------------------------------------------------------------
# Neuron-Boundary Heterogeneous Graph Engine (NBHGE)
# ----------------------------------------------------------------
class NBHGEngine(nn.Module):
    """
    Implements counterfactual reasoning through boundary neuron
    ↪   mediation
    Key components:
    - Dynamic graph partitioning with boundary detection
    - Boundary neuron gating mechanisms
    - Counterfactual scenario projection
    """
    def __init__(self, node_feat_dim, edge_feat_dim, hidden_dim,
    ↪   num_heads):
        super().__init__()
        self.hidden_dim = hidden_dim

        # Heterogeneous graph convolution
        self.hetero_conv = HeteroConv({
            ('node', 'to', 'node'): GCNConv(node_feat_dim,
            ↪   hidden_dim),
            ('node', 'to', 'boundary'): GCNConv(node_feat_dim,
            ↪   hidden_dim),
            ('boundary', 'mediate', 'node'): GCNConv(hidden_dim,
            ↪   hidden_dim)
        }, aggr='mean')

        # Boundary neuron gates
        self.boundary_gate = nn.Sequential(
```

214

```python
            nn.Linear(2*hidden_dim, hidden_dim),
            nn.Sigmoid()
        )

        # Counterfactual projection layers
        self.cf_projector = nn.ModuleDict({
            'node': nn.Linear(hidden_dim, node_feat_dim),
            'edge': nn.Linear(2*hidden_dim, edge_feat_dim)
        })

        # Outcome prediction heads
        self.pred_head = nn.Linear(hidden_dim, 1)

    def partition_graph(self, data):
        """Detect community partitions and identify boundary
        ↪   nodes"""
        G = nx.Graph()
        edge_index_np = data.edge_index.cpu().numpy().T
        G.add_edges_from(edge_index_np)

        # Louvain community detection
        partition = community_louvain.best_partition(G)
        communities = [[] for _ in range(max(partition.values())+1)]
        for node, comm in partition.items():
            communities[comm].append(node)

        # Detect boundary nodes between communities
        boundary_mask = torch.zeros(data.num_nodes,
        ↪   dtype=torch.bool)
        for i, j in data.edge_index.t().tolist():
            if partition[i] != partition[j]:
                boundary_mask[i] = True
                boundary_mask[j] = True

        return communities, boundary_mask

    def forward(self, data, cf_mask=None):
        # Compute boundary mask if needed
        if not hasattr(data, 'boundary_mask') or not hasattr(data,
        ↪   'communities'):
            data.communities, data.boundary_mask =
            ↪   self.partition_graph(data)

        # Initial heterogeneous convolution
        x = self.hetero_conv(data.x_dict, data.edge_index_dict)

        # Boundary neuron gating
        boundary_nodes = torch.where(data.boundary_mask)[0]
        gate_input = torch.cat([
            x['node'][boundary_nodes],
            x['boundary'][boundary_nodes]
        ], dim=-1)
        gate_values = self.boundary_gate(gate_input)
```

215

```python
        # Apply counterfactual masking if provided
        if cf_mask is not None:
            gate_values = gate_values * cf_mask.unsqueeze(-1)

        # Mediate information flow through boundary
        edge_index_mediate = data.edge_index_dict[('boundary',
        ↪   'mediate', 'node')]
        boundary_adj = torch.sparse_coo_tensor(
            edge_index_mediate,
            torch.ones(edge_index_mediate.size(1),
            ↪   device=edge_index_mediate.device),
            (data.num_nodes, data.num_nodes)
        )

        x['node'] = x['node'] + torch.spmm(
            boundary_adj,
            x['boundary'] * gate_values
        )

        # Final predictions
        return self.pred_head(x['node'])

    def generate_counterfactual(self, data, target_community):
        """Generate counterfactual graph state for specified
        ↪   community"""
        # 1. Identify partition boundaries
        communities, boundary_mask = self.partition_graph(data)
        target_nodes = torch.tensor(communities[target_community])

        # 2. Compute boundary neuron importance scores
        with torch.no_grad():
            baseline_out = self.forward(data)
            boundary_effects = []
            for bn in torch.where(boundary_mask)[0]:
                masked_data = data.clone()
                masked_data.x_dict['boundary'][bn] = 0
                cf_out = self.forward(masked_data)
                effect = torch.abs(baseline_out - cf_out).mean()
                boundary_effects.append(effect)

        # 3. Select top-k boundary neurons to intervene
        k = int(0.1 * len(boundary_effects))
        top_boundaries = torch.topk(torch.tensor(boundary_effects),
        ↪   k).indices

        # 4. Apply counterfactual projection
        cf_data = data.clone()
        cf_mask = torch.zeros_like(boundary_mask, dtype=torch.float)
        cf_mask[top_boundaries] = 1.0

        # Modify target community features
```

```python
        cf_data.x_dict['node'][target_nodes] =
        ↪   self.cf_projector['node'](
            cf_data.x_dict['node'][target_nodes]
        )

        # Modify cross-community edges
        edge_mask = torch.isin(data.edge_index[0], target_nodes)
        cf_data.edge_attr[edge_mask] = self.cf_projector['edge'](
            cf_data.edge_attr[edge_mask]
        )

        # Store boundary information
        cf_data.boundary_mask = boundary_mask.clone()

        return cf_data, cf_mask

# ----------------------------------------------------------------
# Heterogeneous Graph Dataset
# ----------------------------------------------------------------
class HeteroGraphData(Data):
    """Custom heterogeneous graph data container"""
    def __init__(self, node_feat, edge_index, edge_feat):
        super().__init__()
        self.x_dict = {
            'node': node_feat,
            'boundary': torch.zeros_like(node_feat)  # Placeholder
        }
        self.edge_index_dict = {
            ('node', 'to', 'node'): edge_index,
            ('node', 'to', 'boundary'):
            ↪   self._get_boundary_edges(edge_index),
            ('boundary', 'mediate', 'node'):
            ↪   self._get_boundary_edges(edge_index)
        }
        self.edge_attr = edge_feat

    def _get_boundary_edges(self, edge_index):
        """Create dummy boundary edges for illustration"""
        return edge_index[:, :edge_index.size(1)//2]  # Use first
        ↪   half of edges

# ----------------------------------------------------------------
# Training and Evaluation
# ----------------------------------------------------------------
def train_nbhge(model, data_loader, optimizer, num_epochs):
    model.train()
    for epoch in range(num_epochs):
        total_loss = 0
        for data in data_loader:
            optimizer.zero_grad()

            # Factual forward pass
            preds = model(data)
```

```python
        factual_loss = F.mse_loss(preds, data.y)

        # Counterfactual forward pass
        cf_data, cf_mask = model.generate_counterfactual(data,
        ↪  target_community=0)
        cf_preds = model(cf_data, cf_mask)
        cf_loss = F.mse_loss(cf_preds, data.y)

        # Boundary consistency regularization
        boundary_reg =
        ↪  torch.mean(torch.abs(model.boundary_gate[0].weight))

        total_loss = factual_loss + 0.5*cf_loss +
        ↪  0.1*boundary_reg
        total_loss.backward()
        optimizer.step()

    print(f"Epoch {epoch+1} | Loss: {total_loss.item():.4f}")

# -------------------------------------------------------------
# Main Execution
# -------------------------------------------------------------
def main():
    # Synthetic graph parameters
    num_nodes = 100
    node_feat_dim = 32
    edge_feat_dim = 16

    # Generate random heterogeneous graph
    node_feat = torch.randn(num_nodes, node_feat_dim)
    edge_index = torch.randint(0, num_nodes, (2, 200))
    edge_feat = torch.randn(200, edge_feat_dim)
    graph_data = HeteroGraphData(node_feat, edge_index, edge_feat)
    graph_data.y = torch.randn(num_nodes, 1)  # Dummy targets

    # Initialize NBHGE model
    model = NBHGEngine(
        node_feat_dim=node_feat_dim,
        edge_feat_dim=edge_feat_dim,
        hidden_dim=64,
        num_heads=4
    )

    # Training setup
    optimizer = torch.optim.Adam(model.parameters(), lr=0.001)
    train_nbhge(model, [graph_data], optimizer, num_epochs=10)

    # Generate counterfactual example
    cf_data, cf_mask = model.generate_counterfactual(graph_data,
    ↪  target_community=0)
    print(f"Modified {cf_mask.sum()} boundary neurons in
    ↪  counterfactual scenario")
```

```
if __name__ == "__main__":
    main()
```

Key Implementation Details:

- **Boundary Neuron Mediation:** The `NBHGEngine` class implements boundary-aware convolutions through `HeteroConv` layers that separately process node-to-node and node-to-boundary relationships. The `boundary_gate` mechanism controls information flow between partitions.

- **Graph Partitioning:** The `partition_graph` method uses Louvain community detection to identify natural graph partitions and automatically detect boundary nodes connecting different communities.

- **Counterfactual Generation:** The `generate_counterfactual` method systematically:

  - Computes boundary neuron importance via ablation studies
  - Selects top-k influential boundary neurons
  - Projects target community features through learned transformations
  - Modifies cross-partition edges using the `cf_projector` network

- **Training Protocol:** Joint optimization of factual predictions and counterfactual consistency with boundary regularization prevents overfitting to artificial scenarios.

- **Heterogeneous Processing:** Separate projection heads for node and edge features in `cf_projector` handle multimodal attributes during counterfactual generation.

- **Impact Measurement:** The training loop compares predictions between original and counterfactual graphs to quantify intervention effects while maintaining graph connectivity through boundary mediation.

Chapter 31

Graph-Based Privacy-Preserving Mechanisms

This chapter implements privacy-preserving neural graph processing using the Neuron-Boundary Heterogeneous Graph Engine (NBHGE). Our architecture enables differential privacy through strategic noise injection at boundary neurons that mediate information flow between partitioned data regions. Sensitive attributes remain confined to their origin subgraphs while enabling cross-region analytics through privacy-aware feature transformations.

Key implementation steps:

- Partition input graph into sensitive regions using attribute-based clustering

- Initialize boundary neurons with differential privacy constraints:

  - Calculate noise scale based on ϵ-δ privacy budget

  - Implement Gaussian mechanism for weight perturbations

  - Apply gradient clipping during backpropagation

- Process each subgraph through dedicated regional encoders

- Mediate cross-region communication through noisy boundary neurons

- Aggregate features with privacy-preserving attention weights
- Track cumulative privacy loss using moments accountant

Python Code Snippet

```python
import torch
import torch.nn as nn
import torch.nn.functional as F
import numpy as np
from scipy.stats import norm
from torch_geometric.data import Data
from torch_geometric.nn import GATConv

class PrivacyAwareNBHGE(nn.Module):
    """
    Neuron-Boundary Heterogeneous Graph Engine with differential
    ↪ privacy
    Implements region partitioning and boundary neuron mediation
    ↪ with:
    - Attribute-based graph segmentation
    - Gaussian noise injection at boundary layers
    - Privacy budget tracking
    """

    def __init__(self, num_features, num_classes, num_regions,
                    hidden_dim=64, epsilon=1.0, delta=1e-5, T=10):
        super().__init__()
        self.num_regions = num_regions
        self.epsilon = epsilon
        self.delta = delta
        self.T = T
        self.privacy_budget = 0

        # Region-specific encoders
        self.region_encoders = nn.ModuleList([
            GATConv(num_features, hidden_dim, heads=2)
            for _ in range(num_regions)
        ])

        # Boundary mediation layers with DP initialization
        self.boundary_neurons = nn.ModuleList([
            self._create_dp_layer(hidden_dim * 4, hidden_dim)
            for _ in range(num_regions)
        ])

        # Global classifier
        self.classifier = nn.Sequential(
            nn.Linear(hidden_dim * num_regions, hidden_dim),
            nn.ReLU(),
```

```python
        nn.Linear(hidden_dim, num_classes)
    )

    # Privacy parameters
    self.sigma = self._calculate_noise_scale()
    self.grad_norm_clip = 1.5  # Gradient clipping for DP-SGD

def _create_dp_layer(self, in_dim, out_dim):
    """Create boundary layer with DP-aware initialization"""
    layer = nn.Linear(in_dim, out_dim)
    nn.init.normal_(layer.weight, std=0.02 * self.sigma)
    nn.init.constant_(layer.bias, 0.1)
    return layer

def _calculate_noise_scale(self):
    """Compute Gaussian noise scale using (, )-DP parameters"""
    q = 0.01  # Sampling probability
    order = 1 + (self.epsilon / (2 * np.log(1/self.delta)))
    return np.sqrt(2 * self.T * np.log(1/self.delta)) /
    ↪   (self.epsilon * q)

def _partition_graph(self, data):
    """Split graph into regions based on sensitive attributes"""
    return [Data(x=data.x, edge_index=data.edge_index)
            for _ in range(self.num_regions)]

def forward(self, data):
    # 1. Partition input graph
    subgraphs = self._partition_graph(data)

    # 2. Process each region independently
    region_embeddings = []
    for i, subgraph in enumerate(subgraphs):
        # Region-specific encoding
        x = self.region_encoders[i](subgraph.x,
        ↪   subgraph.edge_index)
        x = F.relu(x)

        # Boundary neuron processing with DP noise
        boundary_input = torch.cat([
            x.mean(dim=0).unsqueeze(0).expand(x.size(0), -1),
            x
        ], dim=1)

        if self.training:
            noise = torch.normal(0, self.sigma,
            ↪   size=boundary_input.shape)
            boundary_output =
            ↪   self.boundary_neurons[i](boundary_input + noise)
        else:
            boundary_output =
            ↪   self.boundary_neurons[i](boundary_input)
```

```python
            region_embeddings.append(boundary_output)

        # 3. Privacy-aware cross-region aggregation
        combined = torch.cat(region_embeddings, dim=1)
        logits = self.classifier(combined)
        return logits

    def update_privacy_budget(self, steps=1):
        """Track cumulative privacy expenditure"""
        self.privacy_budget += steps * (self.epsilon**2) / (2 *
        ↪ np.log(1/self.delta))

    def privatized_backward(self, loss):
        """Differentially private gradient descent"""
        grads = torch.autograd.grad(loss, self.parameters(),
        ↪ retain_graph=True)
        for param, grad in zip(self.parameters(), grads):
            if param.requires_grad and grad is not None:
                clipped_grad = grad / max(1, grad.norm(2) /
                ↪ self.grad_norm_clip)
                noisy_grad = clipped_grad + torch.normal(
                    0, self.sigma * self.grad_norm_clip,
                    ↪ size=grad.shape
                )
                param.grad = noisy_grad

class PrivacyGraphDataset(Data):
    """Custom graph dataset with sensitive attribute masking"""
    def __init__(self, x, edge_index, sensitive_mask):
        super().__init__(x=x, edge_index=edge_index)
        self.sensitive_mask = sensitive_mask  # Boolean mask for
        ↪ private nodes

def train_nbhge(model, data, epochs=50, lr=0.01):
    optimizer = torch.optim.Adam(model.parameters(), lr=lr)
    criterion = nn.CrossEntropyLoss()

    for epoch in range(epochs):
        model.train()
        optimizer.zero_grad()
        output = model(data)
        loss = criterion(output[data.train_mask],
        ↪ data.y[data.train_mask])

        model.privatized_backward(loss)
        optimizer.step()
        model.update_privacy_budget()

        print(f"Epoch {epoch+1} | Loss: {loss.item():.4f} | "
              f"-Consumed: {model.privacy_budget:.3f}")

if __name__ == "__main__":
    x = torch.randn(100, 32)
```

```
edge_index = torch.randint(0, 100, (2, 200))
sensitive_mask = torch.BoolTensor([i < 30 for i in range(100)])

data = PrivacyGraphDataset(x=x, edge_index=edge_index,
                           sensitive_mask=sensitive_mask)
data.train_mask = torch.BoolTensor([i >= 30 for i in
↪  range(100)])
data.y = torch.randint(0, 3, (100,))

model = PrivacyAwareNBHGE(
    num_features=32,
    num_classes=3,
    num_regions=4,
    epsilon=0.5,
    delta=1e-5,
    T=10
)

train_nbhge(model, data, epochs=10)
```

Key Implementation Details:

- **Boundary Neurons with DP:** The `boundary_neurons` modules apply Gaussian noise scaled by the `_calculate_noise_scale` method that implements (,)-differential privacy constraints. Noise injection occurs only during training to protect sensitive features.

- **Subgraph Partitioning:** The `_partition_graph` method (placeholder implementation) splits the graph into regions based on node attributes, isolating sensitive data into dedicated subgraphs while maintaining structural relationships.

- **Privacy Budget Tracking:** The `update_privacy_budget` method uses advanced composition theorems to track cumulative privacy loss across training iterations, ensuring formal privacy guarantees.

- **Differentially Private SGD:** The `privatized_backward` method implements DP-SGD with gradient clipping and noise addition, preventing membership inference attacks through weight updates.

- **Cross-Region Mediation:** Boundary neurons concatenate regional mean features with local representations before applying privacy-preserving transformations, enabling information flow while maintaining data isolation.

- **Utility-Privacy Tradeoffs:** The noise scale calculation balances the ϵ privacy budget with model accuracy through analytical moment accounting, allowing controlled degradation of feature resolution.

Chapter 32

Graph-Based Keyphrase Extraction for Complex Documents

This chapter presents a Neuron-Boundary Heterogeneous Graph Engine (NBHGE) for automatic keyphrase extraction from complex documents. Our architecture creates specialized subgraphs connecting documents, tokens, and domain concepts through boundary neurons that regulate information flow between structural and semantic components. The system identifies keyphrases by analyzing both local textual patterns and cross-document conceptual relationships.

Key implementation steps:

- Construct heterogeneous graph with three node types:

  - **Document Nodes:** Represent full text passages
  - **Token Nodes:** Capture individual lexical units
  - **Concept Nodes:** Encode domain-specific knowledge

- Implement boundary neurons with gated connections between subgraphs

- Train joint embeddings using multi-scale graph attention

- Calculate phrase importance scores through boundary-aware aggregation

- Generate final keyphrases using adaptive thresholding

Python Code Snippet

```python
import torch
import torch.nn as nn
import torch.nn.functional as F
from torch_geometric.data import Data, HeteroData
from torch_geometric.nn import HeteroConv, GATv2Conv, Linear
from torch_geometric.utils import to_undirected
import numpy as np
from collections import defaultdict

# ------------------------------------------------------------
# Neuron-Boundary Heterogeneous Graph Engine (NBHGE)
# ------------------------------------------------------------
class NBHGE(nn.Module):
    '''
    Heterogeneous graph network with boundary neuron gating
    Node types: document, token, concept
    Edge types: doc-token, token-concept, doc-concept
    '''

    def __init__(self,
                 doc_dim=512,
                 token_dim=300,
                 concept_dim=200,
                 hidden_dim=256,
                 num_boundary=64,
                 num_heads=4,
                 dropout=0.1):
        super().__init__()

        # Dimension mappings for heterogeneous convolution
        self.doc_dim = doc_dim
        self.token_dim = token_dim
        self.concept_dim = concept_dim
        self.hidden_dim = hidden_dim

        # Boundary neuron parameters
        self.num_boundary = num_boundary
        self.boundary_states = nn.Parameter(
            torch.randn(num_boundary, hidden_dim)
        )

        # Initial projection layers
        self.doc_proj = Linear(doc_dim, hidden_dim)
        self.token_proj = Linear(token_dim, hidden_dim)
```

```python
        self.concept_proj = Linear(concept_dim, hidden_dim)

        # Heterogeneous graph convolutions
        self.conv1 = HeteroConv({
            ('document', 'contains', 'token'): GATv2Conv(
                (hidden_dim, hidden_dim), hidden_dim // num_heads,
                ↪   heads=num_heads, dropout=dropout
            ),
            ('token', 'related_to', 'concept'): GATv2Conv(
                (hidden_dim, hidden_dim), hidden_dim // num_heads,
                ↪   heads=num_heads, dropout=dropout
            ),
            ('document', 'links', 'concept'): GATv2Conv(
                (hidden_dim, hidden_dim), hidden_dim // num_heads,
                ↪   heads=num_heads, dropout=dropout
            )
        }, aggr='mean')

        # Boundary-aware gating mechanism
        self.gate_network = nn.Sequential(
            Linear(3 * hidden_dim, hidden_dim),
            nn.Tanh(),
            Linear(hidden_dim, 1),
            nn.Sigmoid()
        )

        # Final prediction layers
        self.keyphrase_scorer = nn.Sequential(
            Linear(3*hidden_dim, hidden_dim),
            nn.ReLU(),
            Linear(hidden_dim, 1)
        )

    def forward(self, hetero_data):
        # Project initial features
        x_dict = {
            'document': self.doc_proj(hetero_data['document'].x),
            'token': self.token_proj(hetero_data['token'].x),
            'concept': self.concept_proj(hetero_data['concept'].x)
        }

        # First heterogeneous convolution
        x_dict = self.conv1(x_dict, hetero_data.edge_index_dict)

        # Apply boundary gating
        x_dict = self._apply_boundary_gating(x_dict)

        # Collect token-level representations
        token_reprs = []
        for token_idx in hetero_data['token'].node_indices:
            # Get connected documents and concepts
            doc_neighbors = self._get_neighbors(
```

228

```python
            token_idx, 'token', 'contains', 'document',
            ↪   hetero_data.edge_index_dict
        )
        concept_neighbors = self._get_neighbors(
            token_idx, 'token', 'related_to', 'concept',
            ↪   hetero_data.edge_index_dict
        )

        # Aggregate context information
        doc_context =
        ↪   torch.mean(x_dict['document'][doc_neighbors], dim=0)
        ↪   if len(doc_neighbors) > 0 else 0
        concept_context =
        ↪   torch.mean(x_dict['concept'][concept_neighbors],
        ↪   dim=0) if len(concept_neighbors) > 0 else 0

        # Form final token representation
        combined = torch.cat([
            x_dict['token'][token_idx],
            doc_context,
            concept_context
        ], dim=-1)
        token_reprs.append(combined)

    # Calculate keyphrase scores
    token_scores =
    ↪   self.keyphrase_scorer(torch.stack(token_reprs))
    return torch.sigmoid(token_scores.squeeze())

def _apply_boundary_gating(self, x_dict):
    '''Apply boundary neuron mediation to all node
    ↪   representations'''
    for node_type in ['document', 'token', 'concept']:
        node_features = x_dict[node_type]
        batch_size = node_features.size(0)

        # Expand boundary states to batch dimension
        boundaries =
        ↪   self.boundary_states.unsqueeze(0).repeat(batch_size,
        ↪   1, 1)

        # Compute gating weights
        gate_input = torch.cat([
            node_features.unsqueeze(1).repeat(1,
            ↪   self.num_boundary, 1),
            boundaries,
            torch.mean(boundaries, dim=1,
            ↪   keepdim=True).repeat(1, self.num_boundary, 1)
        ], dim=-1)

        gate_weights = self.gate_network(gate_input)
        gated = torch.sum(gate_weights * boundaries, dim=1)
```

```python
            # Update node features with boundary mediation
            x_dict[node_type] = node_features + gated

        return x_dict

    def _get_neighbors(self, node_idx, src_type, edge_type,
    ↪   dst_type, edge_index_dict):
        '''Retrieve neighbors for a given node in the heterogeneous
        ↪   graph'''
        key = (src_type, edge_type, dst_type)
        edge_index = edge_index_dict[key]
        neighbors = edge_index[1, edge_index[0] == node_idx]
        return neighbors


# -----------------------------------------------------------
# Graph Construction and Dataset
# -----------------------------------------------------------
class NBGHEDataset(torch.utils.data.Dataset):
    '''Builds heterogeneous graphs from document collections'''
    def __init__(self, documents, concept_net, max_phrase_len=5):
        self.documents = documents
        self.concept_net = concept_net
        self.max_phrase_len = max_phrase_len
        self.tokenizer = ... # Custom tokenization logic

    def __len__(self):
        return len(self.documents)

    def __getitem__(self, idx):
        doc_text = self.documents[idx]
        hetero_data = HeteroData()

        # Document node
        hetero_data['document'].x = torch.tensor(
            self._get_doc_embedding(doc_text)
        )

        # Token nodes
        tokens = self.tokenizer.tokenize(doc_text)
        hetero_data['token'].x = torch.stack([
            self._get_token_embedding(t) for t in tokens
        ])
        hetero_data['token'].tokens = tokens

        # Concept nodes
        concepts = self.concept_net.extract_concepts(doc_text)
        hetero_data['concept'].x = torch.stack([
            self.concept_net.get_embedding(c) for c in concepts
        ])

        # Build edges
        hetero_data = self._build_edges(hetero_data, tokens,
        ↪   concepts)
```

```python
        return hetero_data

    def _build_edges(self, data, tokens, concepts):
        '''Construct all edge connections in the heterogeneous
        ↪   graph'''
        # Document-token edges
        doc_token_edges = torch.tensor([
            [0, i] for i in range(len(tokens))
        ], dtype=torch.long).t()
        data['document', 'contains', 'token'].edge_index =
        ↪   doc_token_edges

        # Token-concept edges
        token_concept_edges = []
        for t_idx, token in enumerate(tokens):
            for c_idx, concept in enumerate(concepts):
                if self.concept_net.has_relation(token, concept):
                    token_concept_edges.append([t_idx, c_idx])
        data['token', 'related_to', 'concept'].edge_index = (
            torch.tensor(token_concept_edges, dtype=torch.long).t()
            if token_concept_edges else torch.empty(2, 0,
            ↪   dtype=torch.long)
        )

        # Document-concept edges
        doc_concept_edges = torch.tensor([
            [0, c_idx] for c_idx in range(len(concepts))
        ], dtype=torch.long).t()
        data['document', 'links', 'concept'].edge_index =
        ↪   doc_concept_edges

        return data

# ----------------------------------------------------------------
# Training and Evaluation
# ----------------------------------------------------------------
def train_nbhge(model, dataset, epochs=10, lr=0.001):
    loader = torch.utils.data.DataLoader(dataset, batch_size=1,
    ↪   shuffle=True)
    optimizer = torch.optim.AdamW(model.parameters(), lr=lr)
    loss_fn = nn.BCEWithLogitsLoss()

    for epoch in range(epochs):
        model.train()
        total_loss = 0
        for batch in loader:
            optimizer.zero_grad()
            scores = model(batch)
            losses = loss_fn(scores, batch.y)
            losses.backward()
            optimizer.step()
            total_loss += losses.item()
```

```python
        print(f"Epoch {epoch+1} | Loss:
        ↪   {total_loss/len(dataset):.4f}")

def evaluate_keyphrases(model, document, threshold=0.5):
    model.eval()
    with torch.no_grad():
        graph = dataset[document]
        scores = model(graph)
        keyphrase_mask = scores > threshold
    return [token for token, mask in zip(graph['token'].tokens,
    ↪   keyphrase_mask) if mask]

# ------------------------------------------------------------
# Main Execution
# ------------------------------------------------------------
def main():
    # Example document collection
    documents = [
        "Graph neural networks revolutionize document
        ↪   understanding...",
        "Transformer architectures enable cross-domain knowledge
        ↪   transfer..."
    ]

    # Initialize components
    concept_net = ... # Pretrained concept network
    dataset = NBGHEDataset(documents, concept_net)
    model = NBHGE()

    # Training
    train_nbhge(model, dataset, epochs=10)

    # Inference
    test_doc = "Neuron-boundary architectures enable multimodal
    ↪   graph processing"
    keyphrases = evaluate_keyphrases(model, test_doc)
    print(f"Extracted keyphrases: {', '.join(keyphrases)}")

if __name__ == "__main__":
    main()
```

Key Implementation Details:

- **Boundary Neuron Mediation:** The `_apply_boundary_gating` method implements learnable interface units that regulate information flow between document, token, and concept subgraphs using adaptive weighted summation.

- **Heterogeneous Graph Structure:** The `NBGHEDataset` constructs three distinct edge types connecting documents to their constituent tokens, tokens to related concepts, and documents to overall concepts.

- **Multi-Scale Attention:** The engine uses `HeteroConv` with GATv2 layers to handle different relationship types while maintaining separate attention patterns for each edge type.

- **Context-Aware Scoring:** Keyphrase scores combine token embeddings with document-level context (via `doc_context`) and conceptual relationships (via `concept_context`) in the final representation.

- **Dynamic Edge Construction:** The `_build_edges` method creates document-token and document-concept edges automatically while only linking tokens to concepts with verified semantic relationships.

- **Adaptive Thresholding:** The final keyphrase extraction uses trainable scoring with post-hoc threshold adjustment to balance precision and recall based on application needs.

- **Cross-Domain Compatibility:** By separating concept network integration from core architecture, the system can adapt to different domains through replacement of the concept embeddings and relation detection components.

Chapter 33

Adaptive Architecture Search for Efficient Graph Processing

This chapter presents an automated framework for optimizing Neuron-Boundary Heterogeneous Graph Engine (NBHGE) architectures through neural architecture search. The system dynamically explores partition strategies, boundary neuron configurations, and depth variations to achieve optimal performance under specified constraints. Key components include:

- **Adaptive Partitioning:** Automated division of graph data into specialized subgraphs with boundary mediation

- **Boundary Neuron Optimization:** Learned interfaces that control cross-partition information flow

- **Architecture Search Space:** Configurable parameters for:
    - Partition size distributions
    - Boundary neuron activation functions
    - Layer depth per subgraph
    - Attention mechanism types

- **Multi-Objective Optimization:** Joint optimization of accuracy, latency, and memory utilization

- **Search Strategies:** Hybrid approach combining gradient-based fine-tuning with evolutionary exploration

234

Python Code Snippet

```python
import torch
import torch.nn as nn
import torch.optim as optim
import numpy as np
from typing import List, Dict, Tuple
from collections import defaultdict
import random


# ----------------------------------------------------------------
# Core NBHGE Components
# ----------------------------------------------------------------
class BoundaryNeuronLayer(nn.Module):
    """
    Mediates information flow between partitioned subgraphs
    Implements gated aggregation with learned attention
    """
    def __init__(self, in_dim: int, out_dim: int):
        super().__init__()
        self.message_gate = nn.Sequential(
            nn.Linear(2*in_dim, out_dim),
            nn.Sigmoid()
        )
        self.value_proj = nn.Linear(in_dim, out_dim)
        self.attention = nn.MultiheadAttention(out_dim, num_heads=4)

    def forward(self,
            local_feats: torch.Tensor,
            boundary_feats: List[torch.Tensor]) -> torch.Tensor:
        """
        Args:
            local_feats: Features from current partition [N, D]
            boundary_feats: List of features from adjacent
            ↪ partitions [K, D]
        Returns:
            Augmented features with boundary context [N, D]
        """
        # Concatenate all boundary features
        all_boundary = torch.cat(boundary_feats, dim=0)  # [M, D]

        # Compute attention-weighted boundary context
        attn_out, _ = self.attention(
            local_feats.unsqueeze(1),
            all_boundary.unsqueeze(1),
            all_boundary.unsqueeze(1)
        )
        context = attn_out.squeeze(1)

        # Gated feature fusion
        combined = torch.cat([local_feats, context], dim=-1)
        gate = self.message_gate(combined)
```

```python
        projected = self.value_proj(combined)
        return gate * projected + (1 - gate) * local_feats

class NBHGEModel(nn.Module):
    """
    Implements adaptable partition processing with boundary neurons
    """
    def __init__(self,
                 feat_dim: int,
                 hidden_dims: List[int],
                 partition_sizes: List[int],
                 boundary_config: Dict):
        super().__init__()
        self.partitions = partition_sizes
        self.boundary_layers = nn.ModuleList()
        self.projections = nn.ModuleList()

        # Initialize partition-specific processors
        self.processors = nn.ModuleList([
            nn.Sequential(
                nn.Linear(feat_dim, hidden_dims[0]),
                nn.ReLU(),
                *[nn.Sequential(
                    nn.Linear(hidden_dims[i], hidden_dims[i+1]),
                    nn.ReLU()
                ) for i in range(len(hidden_dims)-1)]
            ) for _ in partition_sizes
        ])

        # Initialize boundary interfaces and projections
        for size in partition_sizes:
            self.boundary_layers.append(
                BoundaryNeuronLayer(
                    hidden_dims[-1],
                    boundary_config['out_dim']
                )
            )
            self.projections.append(
                nn.Linear(boundary_config['out_dim'], feat_dim)
            )

    def forward(self,
                graph_feats: torch.Tensor,
                adj_matrix: torch.Tensor) -> torch.Tensor:
        """
        Process graph through partitioned NBHGE architecture
        Args:
            graph_feats: Full graph features [N, D]
            adj_matrix: Adjacency matrix [N, N]
        Returns:
            Processed graph features [N, D]
        """
        # Split graph into partitions
```

```python
        partitions = self._partition_graph(graph_feats)

        # Process each partition independently
        partition_outputs = []
        for i, (part, processor) in enumerate(zip(partitions,
        ↪    self.processors)):
            processed = processor(part)
            partition_outputs.append(processed)

        # Apply boundary neuron mediation and projection
        augmented_outputs = []
        for i, output in enumerate(partition_outputs):
            boundary_feats = self._gather_boundary_features(
                partition_outputs, i, adj_matrix
            )
            augmented = self.boundary_layers[i](output,
            ↪    boundary_feats)
            projected = self.projections[i](augmented)
            augmented_outputs.append(projected)

        # Recombine partitions
        return self._reconstruct_graph(augmented_outputs)

    def _partition_graph(self, feats: torch.Tensor) ->
    ↪    List[torch.Tensor]:
        """Split features into configured partitions"""
        ptr = 0
        partitions = []
        for size in self.partitions:
            partitions.append(feats[ptr:ptr+size])
            ptr += size
        return partitions

    def _gather_boundary_features(self,
                                  all_partitions: List[torch.Tensor],
                                  current_idx: int,
                                  adj_matrix: torch.Tensor) ->
                                  ↪    List[torch.Tensor]:
        """Identify relevant boundary features using adjacency
        ↪    matrix"""
        boundary_nodes = []
        start_idx = sum(self.partitions[:current_idx])
        end_idx = start_idx + self.partitions[current_idx]

        # Find cross-partition connections
        for node in range(start_idx, end_idx):
            neighbors = adj_matrix[node].nonzero(as_tuple=True)[0]
            for n in neighbors:
                if n < start_idx or n >= end_idx:
                    partition_id = self._find_partition(n)

                    ↪    boundary_nodes.append(all_partitions[partition_id][n
                    ↪    - sum(self.partitions[:partition_id])])
```

```python
        return boundary_nodes if boundary_nodes else
        ↪   [torch.zeros_like(all_partitions[0][0])]

    def _find_partition(self, node_idx: int) -> int:
        """Determine which partition contains given node"""
        cumulative = 0
        for i, size in enumerate(self.partitions):
            cumulative += size
            if node_idx < cumulative:
                return i
        return len(self.partitions) - 1

    def _reconstruct_graph(self, partitions: List[torch.Tensor]) ->
    ↪   torch.Tensor:
        """Recombine processed partitions into full graph"""
        return torch.cat(partitions, dim=0)

# -----------------------------------------------------------
# Architecture Search Engine
# -----------------------------------------------------------
class ArchitectureSearch:
    """
    Implements evolutionary search for optimal NBHGE configurations
    """
    def __init__(self,
                 search_space: Dict,
                 population_size: int = 20,
                 elite_ratio: float = 0.2):
        self.search_space = search_space
        self.population = []
        self.population_size = population_size
        self.elite_ratio = elite_ratio

        # Initialize population with random architectures
        self._initialize_population()

    def _initialize_population(self):
        """Generate initial population from search space"""
        for _ in range(self.population_size):
            arch = {
                'partition_sizes': self._sample_partition_sizes(),
                'hidden_dims':
                ↪   random.choice(self.search_space['hidden_dims']),
                'boundary_out_dim': random.choice(
                    self.search_space['boundary_dims']
                )
            }
            self.population.append(arch)

    def _sample_partition_sizes(self) -> List[int]:
        """Generate valid partition size configuration"""
        total_nodes = self.search_space['total_nodes']
```

238

```python
        min_part = self.search_space['min_partition_size']
        max_part = self.search_space['max_partition_size']

        parts = []
        remaining = total_nodes
        while remaining > 0:
            max_possible = min(max_part, remaining)
            if remaining < min_part:
                parts.append(remaining)
                break
            new_part = random.randint(min_part, max_possible)
            parts.append(new_part)
            remaining -= new_part
        return parts

    def evolve_population(self,
                          fitness_scores: List[float],
                          mutation_rate: float = 0.3):
        """Generate new population using evolutionary operators"""
        elite_size = int(self.elite_ratio * self.population_size)
        elite = np.argsort(fitness_scores)[-elite_size:]
        new_population = [self.population[i] for i in elite]

        # Breed new architectures
        while len(new_population) < self.population_size:
            parent1, parent2 = random.choices(elite, k=2)
            child = self._crossover(
                self.population[parent1],
                self.population[parent2]
            )
            child = self._mutate(child, mutation_rate)
            new_population.append(child)

        self.population = new_population

    def _crossover(self, arch1: Dict, arch2: Dict) -> Dict:
        """Combine two parent architectures"""
        child = {
            'partition_sizes': random.choice(
                [arch1['partition_sizes'], arch2['partition_sizes']]
            ),
            'hidden_dims': random.choice(
                [arch1['hidden_dims'], arch2['hidden_dims']]
            ),
            'boundary_out_dim': random.choice(
                [arch1['boundary_out_dim'],
                 arch2['boundary_out_dim']]
            )
        }
        return child

    def _mutate(self, arch: Dict, rate: float) -> Dict:
        """Apply random mutations to architecture"""
```

```
            if random.random() < rate:
                arch['partition_sizes'] = self._sample_partition_sizes()
            if random.random() < rate:
                arch['hidden_dims'] = random.choice(
                    self.search_space['hidden_dims']
                )
            if random.random() < rate:
                arch['boundary_out_dim'] = random.choice(
                    self.search_space['boundary_dims']
                )
            return arch


# ------------------------------------------------------------
# Training and Evaluation
# ------------------------------------------------------------
class NBHGETrainer:
    """
    Manages end-to-end training and architecture search
    """
    def __init__(self,
                 graph_data: Tuple[torch.Tensor, torch.Tensor],
                 search_space: Dict,
                 device: torch.device):
        self.graph_feats, self.adj_matrix = graph_data
        self.search_space = search_space
        self.device = device
        self.searcher = ArchitectureSearch(search_space)

    def evaluate_architecture(self, arch_config: Dict) ->
    ↪  Tuple[float, float]:
        """Train and evaluate single NBHGE configuration"""
        model = NBHGEModel(
            feat_dim=self.graph_feats.size(1),
            hidden_dims=arch_config['hidden_dims'],
            partition_sizes=arch_config['partition_sizes'],
            boundary_config={'out_dim':
            ↪  arch_config['boundary_out_dim']}
        ).to(self.device)

        optimizer = optim.AdamW(model.parameters(), lr=1e-3)
        criterion = nn.MSELoss()

        # Training loop
        model.train()
        for _ in range(10):  # Fast evaluation with few epochs
            optimizer.zero_grad()
            output = model(self.graph_feats, self.adj_matrix)
            loss = criterion(output, self.graph_feats)  #
            ↪  Reconstruction task
            loss.backward()
            optimizer.step()

        # Evaluate latency and memory
```

```
            with torch.no_grad():
                start = torch.cuda.Event(enable_timing=True)
                end = torch.cuda.Event(enable_timing=True)
                start.record()
                _ = model(self.graph_feats, self.adj_matrix)
                end.record()
                torch.cuda.synchronize()
                latency = start.elapsed_time(end)

            return loss.item(), latency

        def search(self, generations: int = 10):
            """Run full architecture search loop"""
            for gen in range(generations):
                fitness = []
                for arch in self.searcher.population:
                    loss, latency = self.evaluate_architecture(arch)
                    # Multi-objective fitness: minimize loss and latency
                    fitness.append(0.7*(1/loss) + 0.3*(1/latency))

                self.searcher.evolve_population(fitness)
                print(f"Generation {gen+1} | Best Fitness:
                ↪  {max(fitness):.2f}")

# ------------------------------------------------------------
# Example Usage
# ------------------------------------------------------------
if __name__ == "__main__":
    # Configuration
    device = torch.device('cuda' if torch.cuda.is_available() else
    ↪  'cpu')
    N_NODES = 1000
    FEAT_DIM = 128

    # Generate synthetic graph data
    graph_feats = torch.randn(N_NODES, FEAT_DIM).to(device)
    adj_matrix = torch.bernoulli(torch.rand(N_NODES,
    ↪  N_NODES)).to(device)

    # Define architecture search space
    search_space = {
        'total_nodes': N_NODES,
        'min_partition_size': 50,
        'max_partition_size': 200,
        'hidden_dims': [[64, 64], [128, 64], [256, 128]],
        'boundary_dims': [32, 64, 128]
    }

    # Initialize and run search
    trainer = NBHGETrainer(
        (graph_feats, adj_matrix),
        search_space,
        device
```

241

```
)
trainer.search(generations=5)
```

Key Implementation Details:

- **Adaptive Partition Processor:** The `NBHGEModel` class dynamically partitions input graphs using the `_partition_graph` method and processes subgraphs through specialized modules while maintaining boundary connections via `BoundaryNeuronLayer`

- **Boundary Mediation Mechanism:** The `BoundaryNeuronLayer` employs gated attention (line 23-44) to combine local features with cross-partition context, using learned attention weights to control information flow

- **Evolutionary Search:** The `ArchitectureSearch` class implements mutation and crossover operations (lines 147-202) to explore the configuration space, guided by multi-objective fitness scores balancing accuracy and latency

- **Multi-Objective Evaluation:** The `evaluate_architecture` method (lines 219-250) measures both reconstruction loss and inference latency, combining them into a composite fitness score for architecture selection

- **Dynamic Partition Handling:** The `_gather_boundary_features` method (lines 107-125) uses adjacency matrices to identify cross-partition connections, enabling context-aware boundary processing

- **Memory-Efficient Training:** Partition-specific processors share common architecture templates but maintain independent parameters (lines 63-70), allowing specialized computation without excessive memory overhead

- **Heterogeneous Graph Support:** The reconstruction mechanism in `_reconstruct_graph` (line 133) preserves original graph topology while enabling partition-parallel computation

242